Old Henbury

Marguerite Tonkin

redcliffe

First published in 1999 by
Redcliffe Press Ltd
81g, Pembroke Road, Bristol BS8 3EA

Telephone 0117 9737207

ISBN 1 900178 91 5

This book is dedicated to the families of Henbury, especially the children.

British Cataloguing-in-Publication Data.
A catalogue record for this book is available from the
British Library.

Typeset by Mayhew Typesetting, Rhayader, Powys and
printed by WBC Print, Bridgend.

CONTENTS

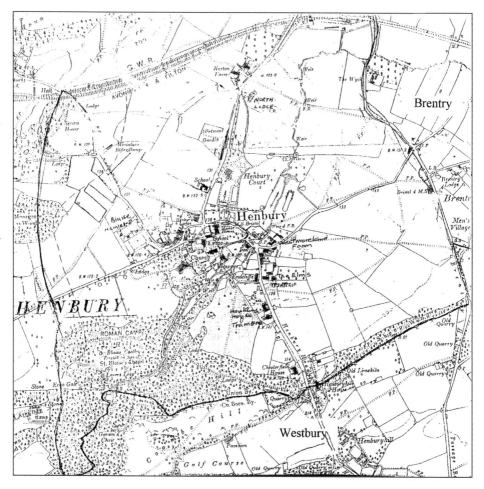

Henbury in 1930.

Introduction

A previous book, *Lost Farms of Henbury* looks at farming in old Henbury including aspects of the farmers' work and social life. It also explains why, in 1950, Henbury began to be transformed into a Bristol suburb.

Old Henbury is written mainly from the reminiscences of villagers, most of whom are now growing old, but ready and willing to contribute to this small account of Henbury as it was in their youth.

Theirs was a largely self-contained community because, in most cases, incomes were small, and outside communications sparse. There was an occasional country bus; and a passenger train from Filton to Avonmouth stopped at Henbury Station. If one did not own a horse, one biked or walked.

Two other small villages, Hallen and Brentry, were closely associated with Henbury. As well as having close family ties, Brentry people came to Henbury Church and schools. Hallen children, when they were seven years old used to progress from their own local Infants' School to the Henbury Boys' and Henbury Girls' Schools. There was a Hallen and Henbury Flower Show, Football Club and W.I.

Westbury village was much larger and with many more shops. Westbury grocers would deliver weekly orders to the smaller villages by horse-drawn vans. From Westbury war memorial, trams provided a service into Bristol and its suburbs.

The ancient Parish of Henbury included Hallen and Brentry, and many other villages besides, and extended right into the Bristol Channel! It is, however Henbury village that is the main subject of this book. We define it roughly within the boundaries of Passage Road to the east, Westbury to the south, the railway to the north and the woodlands of Blaise to the west.

These boundaries are themselves still of interest. From the top of Henbury hill, one can look over to Westbury on Trym, and back down to Henbury, two villages with intertwined histories.

To the east, Passage Road separated Henbury from Brentry. Starting in the heart of Westbury village, it led to roads to New Passage and Old Passage where, in the eighteen and nineteenth centuries, one could take a ferry passage to Wales. To the north, an early twentieth-century branch line of the G.W.R. conveying passengers between Filton and Avonmouth was used by Henbury workers to get to Avonmouth Docks. Blaise Estate dominated the west. For hundreds of years it was in private hands until, in 1926, it became public parkland and beautiful wooded valleys for all to enjoy.

Until 1935, Henbury and its neighbours were a far-flung part of Gloucestershire, rural, quiet, locked into traditions of the past.

From ancient times, like all good old villages, ours had a main road running through its heart. Henbury Road entered the village from Westbury at the hill-top boundary, swept down between farm fields on the right, and large houses backed by the 'Royalls' on the left. It forded the brook by the Salutation Inn, passed the ends of Crow Lane and Station Road, made a sweep left between high stone walls, passed Blaise Castle House gates, and joined the Hallen Road. Hallen Road led past Blaise Hamlet, and curved left to reach Ison hill and the cottages. Nearby were Severn House, Hillend and the railway 'halt'.

Only three roads led off the main one. They were Kings Weston Road leading to the hamlet of Lawrence Weston, and to Sea Mills and Shirehampton. Station Road led to Cribbs Causeway and Passage Road. The third road was Crow Lane, narrow and muddy, leading to the Crow Inn and the hamlet of Brentry.

Our village had a stream, variously known as Hazel Brook, Henbury Trym or simply 'Hen'. Running from north east to south west, it crossed Henbury Road at the ford. Road and stream together made a diagonal cross shape on the map. The farms took up most of the land north and east of Henbury Road (with the exception of Henbury Court), south and west of the road contained large private houses, Blaise Castle Estate and Hamlet.

Where river and road intersect, a lane led to the Parish Church of St. Mary, to the vicarage, to the Boys' School, the Close and Church Lane: in short, to the heart of the village leading the villagers into the centre.

1 – The Heart of the Village

A small anecdote sets the scene for this book about old Henbury. Farmer Tom Hignell recalls:

"I was, in about 1980, invited by a teacher at Henbury School to talk to her class about my farming. She told the children that their school, probably the most important building in the village, had been built on my farm fields. Now, I grant you that education is important, but I believe that there is something more important. With the teacher's permission, I led the children to a vantage point, and, pointing westward asked, 'What is that stone tower? It just shows above the tress. *That* is the most important building in Henbury, and has been for nine hundred years!'"

Tom's anecdote illustrates how the village people of his generation regarded their church. It was the hub of their religious and social life. The seasons of the year and the seasons of their lives were celebrated at their parish church. They were christened, confirmed, married and buried there. They celebrated great religious events: Advent, Christmas, Lent, Easter and Whitsunday. They gave thanks at Rogationtide, at Harvest. They gave thanks for the birth of their babies and for the lives of their old people. There was great enjoyment in singing in the choir on Sundays, at weddings and at choir practice. Social functions at church included the Mothers' Union, Communicants' Guild, a drama club, whist drives and bell-ringing. Church was where you did all these things in the company of your friends. It was where you were happy, and it created a sense of community, a sense of belonging.

To reach the church, parishioners could come from three different directions. One was from the direction of the ford, passing the gates of Henbury Awdelett on the right and the entrance to the vicarage on the left. At the top of the lane, four steps led to the churchyard. Turning right, rounding the corner of the church, passing the obelisk that forms a memorial to the Egyptologist, Amelia Edwardes, brought them to the north porch. Very close to this door is the grave of Scipio Africanus. 'Born a Pagan and a Slave . . .' So reads part of his epitaph.

A second route to the church was to come from the 'Royalls' by way of a tunnel under the vicarage garden into the churchyard opposite the south porch.

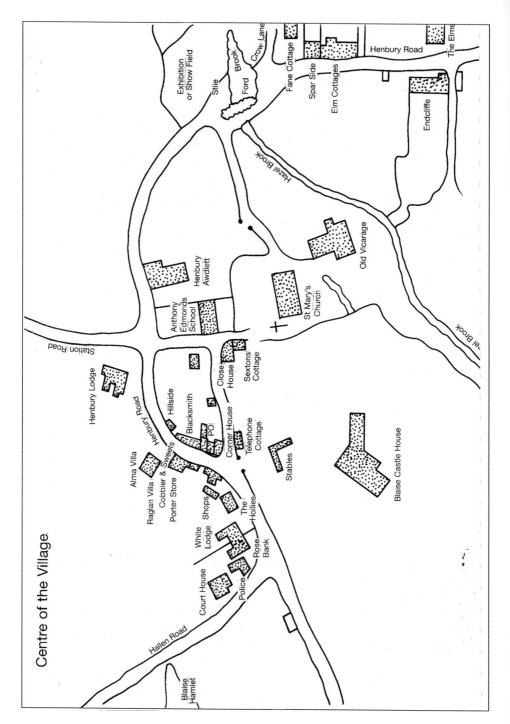

Centre of the Village.

Exhibition or Show Field

Stile

Brook

Ford

Crow Lane

Fane Cottage

Spar Side

Elm Cottages

Henbury Road

The Elms

Endcliffe

Hazel Brook

Henbury Awdlett

Anthony Edmonds School

Old Vicarage

St Mary's Church

Hazel Brook

Station Road

Henbury Lodge

Hillside

Blacksmith

Close House

Sextons Cottage

Henbury Road

P.O.

Corner House

Telephone Cottage

Alma Villa

Raglan Villa

Cobbler & Sweets

Porter Store

Shops

The Hollies

Stables

Blaise Castle House

White Lodge

Rose Bank

Court House

Police

Hallen Road

Blaise Hamlet

The third approach was from Church Lane, through iron gates to the north porch again.

Once inside the church, there is much evidence for the history of Henbury and of its wealthier residents from memorial stones and dedications. The building itself tells its own story. From *Kelly's Directory* 1931, one learns that the nave dates from the reign of King Stephen 1135–1154, that the south chapel was build in the reign of Henry III 1216–1272. Rebuilding and restoration spanned a great length of time, for it was last extensively refurbished in 1878. Greater detail may be read in the leaflet, *St. Mary's Church, Henbury A Brief History.*

In the churchyard, there is more to discover, for here are headstones erected in memory of villagers of all walks of life, and a fine war memorial in honour of soldiers who died in the Great War.

Just inside the iron railings is the Vestry Hall, used for vesting and for vestry meetings and once the site of the thirteenth-century vicarage. Just outside the railings, is the sexton's Cottage. The sexton was in charge of the care of churchyard and church, and also often the duties of bell-ringing and grave-digging. Living next to the church enabled him to keep a look-out for vandals (a nuisance in those days too), and to be up early to ring the bell for service.

Farmer Ray says that his family, like other village families, have for generations attended St. Mary's Church. He recalls that, when he took on Westmoreland Farm as a very young man with his aunt keeping house for him, "Aunt Doll was still very involved, as she had lived, worked and worshipped in the village all her life. I accompanied her to church whenever farm work permitted. Later, as a family man, the whole family could be seen at church every Sunday. Our ancestors were christened and married at St. Mary's for generations, and now lie buried in the churchyard."

Farmer Tom adds: "Ever since mum and dad took the lease of Norton Farm many years ago, when Laura, Bob and I were very small, we have been part of St. Mary's Church, joining in just about everything."

Other villagers happily reminisce about those 'between-the-wars' years in the church choir, Harold in the twenties, Peter in the thirties and forties and David in the forties. Deep in their memories are school outings, choir outings, choir practice. They normally joined the choir aged about eight. Practice was at 7pm on Thursdays when, in Harold's day, they received a half-penny. For the 11am Sunday service and also for evening service they were paid one penny for full attendance. They

9

St Mary's Church, Henbury.

The church bells.

thoroughly enjoyed their choir singing. Peter remarked that he retained an involvement in music and singing well into adulthood.

Fred Talbot also served in the choir with Peter and David, eventually, with Peter, becoming Head choirboys of a 'great choir.' There were sixteen boys and eight men. The organist and choir master at that time was Mr Ransome. The vicar was the Rev. J.C. Lloyd.

Fred and his family lived at Henbury Lodge in Kings Weston Road. His father was sidesman and server, regularly serving at the 7am Communion.

David's father had been a choirman at Henbury for some time before the family moved from Westbury to Henbury.

Some of their other colleagues were Bob and Gordon Steer, Peter Baguley, Brian Frost, Raymond Harris, Percy Furber and two McFarlane cousins from Coombe Dingle. In David's day, the boys were paid quarterly, depending on attendance, behaviour, etc ten to fifteen shillings. Weddings merited an additional payment.

So Church Close was well frequented. It was the main route through to Crow Lane and Henbury hill. All week round, the church was in use for Sunday services, choir practice, weekday services and functions. The sexton was much in evidence outside his house or in the churchyard. Boys arrived at and departed from school. People visited graves to replenish flowers. In the Vestry Hall a registrar (Mr James Addis in 1930) attended on Mondays 1–2pm to register births and deaths. Vestry meetings were held in the hall, vestments stored and collections counted, a useful busy building.

The shops were nearby. The Close provided a short cut for shoppers. The war memorial erected after 1918 was quite appropriately sited here at the centre of village life.

The Boys' School from church tower in 1889.

Sexton's Cottage and Close House.

2 – Church Close

The Boys' School

The grey stone building now used as the village hall has this inscription over the door: FOUNDED by Anthony Edmonds Merchant 1624 REBUILT 1830 by Thomas Stock Esq. Treasurer.

Farmer Tom has an interesting tale to tell about Anthony Edmonds, something like this: "Because he thought his sons to be prodigal, this merchant cut them out of his will in favour of an educational charity. The sons found out and repented, improving their way of life. After their father's death, the will was found to be in the sons' favour; but was contested and deemed a forgery because it was said to have been signed by the 'dead hand' of Anthony Edmonds."

From that time on, boys were eligible for teaching and instruction at his school if they were born within Henbury, Westbury, Horfield, Redwick, Northwick or Aust. From the early days, many clergy of St. Mary's church were successively closely associated with the school. Over time the curriculum varied, sometimes grammar was taught, at other times the three 'Rs'. The children wore blue jackets with the initials AE sewn on like a badge. As a result, they came to be known as the 'Blue Boys'.

(Thomas Stock, sugar refiner, mentioned as 'Treasurer' when the school was rebuilt in 1830 had, about that time, bought the Great House. He soon had it demolished, replacing it with the mansion he called Henbury Court, which in course of time gave way to the new Infant and Junior schools.)

By 1898, the buildings were being used for a Boys' Elementary School, retaining its clerical association by becoming a church school. The Anthony Edmonds Trust funds were then converted to boarding scholarships to some of Bristol's schools.

Most of the boys from the village and from Henbury Parish attended the Boys' Elementary School in the Close. They were there from seven to fourteen years of age. After the Second World War, the leaving age was raised to fifteen. A few of the boys at eleven plus won scholarships to the City grammar schools. All 'old boys' bear witness to the great activity in

13

The Blue Boys, May 1888.

Church Close. Boys would arrive on foot, bicycle, farm cart from nearby and from miles around the parish. At playtime, they would spill out onto the playground. The whole school attended church at festivals and other special occasions.

The inside of the school building has been described by Fred Talbot: "There was no upper floor, just a very high ceiling. You entered the hallway and there was a classroom on the right hand side. Then the large hall was partitioned and held three classes. The lavatories were outside. The present car park was part playground (near the school) and part allotments."

Headmasters and The Close House

Harold Godfrey's headmaster was Mr Harrison, Fred Talbot remembers that his was Mr D Smart. David Hellen writes: "In The Church Close House lived Mr Dennis Smart, his wife and two daughters. His daughters also became school teachers."

Mr Muschamp was appointed headmaster of Henbury Church of England School in 1952, and remained there until shortly before it closed. Although his tenure lies beyond the period to be covered by this book, the description by his widow of house, customs and traditions had remained the same for many years. Hannah Muschamp also gives interesting insights into her experiences as headmaster's wife in a nearly-forgotten age:

"We were asked to look at The Close House as it was then the headmaster's house and went with the job. We looked and were horrified to see a six-bedroomed mansion, with dining room, sitting room and a tiny chapel in the corner (still there), a butler's pantry and a kitchen and scullery all painted dark brown and bottle-green. We thought of our Utility furniture (basic and all that was then available), and declined to live there; though the saving grace to us was the lovely walled garden at the back.

"The house had originally been used as a boarding house for the Anthony Edmonds School opposite. The boys slept at the top and the headmaster down below. When we saw the house, there was a very large bedroom 25ft × 26ft at the top, lit by two very small dormer windows with bars across them. There was a wooden rack across an alcove. This rack had six round holes in it that had been used by the boys for their washing bowls. There was a heavy oak door, also barred with a huge lock – and the keys were still there! The tiny chapel in the sitting room alcove had pretty stained glass windows, a carved surround and a built-in seat at one side. It must have been used for morning prayers.

"When we declined to live there, a group of trustees who were all church members guaranteed £100 each to convert the house into a maisonette and a flat, and to divide the garden into two. We accepted the maisonette and moved in in 1952."

Mrs Muschamp goes on to describe her husband's responsibilities: "My husband's school consisted of three buildings, the Boys' School, in Church Close, the Girls' School in Station Road, and, when school numbers increased, two further classrooms were opened in the Petty Sessions building in Hallen Road (complete with a cell for bad behaviour!). My husband was very fit chasing between the three! At that time, children from Compton Greenfield, Pill, Hallen, Northwick came by bus. An eagle eye was kept on them by Mrs Joyner who also helped to cook school dinners which were served in the Girls' School.

"As it was a church school, my husband had to be a confirmed church member. Morning assemblies were obligatory, and were generally taken by the vicar. All the children went to church on Saints' Days and then had a day off. Carol services were much looked forward to, rehearsals starting in September!

"Then there were prize days, a very complicated procedure, as prizes were given by various trusts. There was Ann Smyth for needlework, Sandford and Gray 2/6d for a pair of boots plus a piece of china to mothers whose children had given complete attendance (I still have a Denby jug I was given). Church Land Trust gave books which are still given now to Northwick, Henbury Court and Brentry Schools."

In her role as headmaster's wife, she was impressed by some of her new experiences:

"My first memory of Henbury – I was sitting at one of the dormer windows watching files of children circling the church. It was Ascension Day and they were following the custom of 'clipping the church', and singing, 'We love this place, Oh God'. As the numbers of pupils increased, there was a double circle of children. Sadly when the school closed, this lovely old custom died too.

"As headmaster's wife, my life changed completely. We had three dear old ladies living in Beaconsfield House, and I was rather nonplussed to receive a calling card, and was summoned to take tea with them. Wearing white gloves, my small daughter in her best frock, we were given a third degree in the nicest possible way.

"The Close House wasn't the warmest of houses, it was a question of 'first up lit the fire'. Two children and husband went off to school – and they were all back at 12 for lunch, back at 4 for tea. No latchkeys for them!

"I was immediately roped in to take over the Mothers' Union, which I hadn't even heard of! Then, once a year I was detailed off to empty all the Children's Society boxes, which were shaped like little beds and were 'swine' to open – it took me a day to cycle round all of Henbury, that is before the Estate grew. I then joined the W.I, which was held in the Hallen Hut – it boasted a tortoise shell stove. If you were lucky you roasted to death; if not, you were frozen to death.

"My children were soon absorbed too. Peter sung in the choir which meant we all went to church twice every Sunday. He joined the Scouts. Jenny was a Brownie. The Boys' School was a hive of industry day and night.

"The big event of the year was the Christmas Fair. All the school desks etc were put in the playground and covered with tarpaulins; and the church elders moved in to prepare for the big event. There were many rich families in Henbury, and an enormous amount of money was raised. I have lost count of the jars of jam, bath salts I have pushed into pretty jars, cakes I have made and dolls I have dressed. We worked the whole year through, and got a great deal of satisfaction out of the end result. I wonder how many children got piles from sitting on damp desks the following Monday? And the poor caretaker must have got a hernia from all the pushing and pulling he did!

"Looking back, I realise now that the focal point of our life was the village and the church. We did feel that we were part of a community; and I think that was why we all felt so sad when the church school had to close.

"My husband opened Henbury Court School in 1956. The church school carried on for a little while but as the Estate grew, so did the number of children, and the church school couldn't cope any more."

Mrs Muschamp visited Henbury Court's fortieth anniversary. She writes: "I was so pleased to see that some of the old traditions are still around."

This is an extract from a Henbury Conservation Society leaflet dated about 1987:

The Close House owned by Anthony Edmonds Trust was used as the Schoolmaster's house for over three hundred years. It may have been built as early as 1585 – forty years before the Charity was founded.

Sexton's Cottage

Joined to The Close House and next to the church gate and Vestry Hall, Sexton's Cottage is believed to date from at least the seventeenth century.

Tom and Ray have clear memories of Sexton/Verger Devenish, a bilingual Channel Islander. But David and Peter best remember that the verger in their youth was Mr Harry Baguley, successor to Mr Devenish. Harry Baguley lived at Sexton's Cottage with his wife and children, Peter and Mary. Peter Baguley was a friend of Peter Powesland who recalls: "We, the two Peters, would play sometimes noisily in the churchyard which Peter Baguley regarded as his garden. But my father disapproved of this as being unseemly, and also too near his employer's house (Dr Wills of The Old Vicarage). Peter Baguley, when he grew up, trained as an actor, at Bristol Old Vic Theatre School. Later, he joined the BBC and became a presenter in Belfast." Mary Baguley was a great friend of Betty Woodsford when they were pupils together at the Girls' School in Station Road.

Someone who evidently knew Mr Harry Baguley well is mentioned in Doreen Layzell's book, *Invitation to Henbury*. Here is an extract: "Joseph Gould, (North porch St. Mary's) died 1946 aged 78. Rang church bells every Sunday for 64 years wearing black bowler and gaiters. He was a grain checker at Avonmouth. Mr Gould taught Mr Baguley, verger and grave digger to ring bells. On New Year's Eve, these two men and other ringers would repair to the tap room, Porter Stores. When refreshed, a right merry peal was rung. At other times, cider, bought from Westmoreland Farm, was drunk down the stoke hole in the church."

A further witness that Church and Close were full of life in those grand old days!

3 – Antiquity of Henbury

St. Mary's Church is the oldest building still standing in the village, and with an even older foundation. However, archaeological evidence suggests the presence of people in the vicinity further back again, to Neolithic times when farmers worked on the Blaise Castle Estate.

To complement written evidence of Henbury's antiquity, there are a number of artefacts at the Blaise Castle House Museum. Also, a fairly recent Henbury resident, Mr David Hough has discovered, dug up and collected many such objects here in the village, a small selection of which has been photographed for this book.

In *A Popular Retreat* one reads that there is also evidence of Bronze Age settlers 1800–800 B.C., and of Iron Age communities on King's Weston Hill and Blaise Castle Hill 800 B.C.–A.D. 43.

During the period of Roman occupation A.D. 43–410 there were communities on Kings Weston and Blaise Castle Hills, and a Roman road running from Gloucester to the old Roman port at Sea Mills. Cribbs Causeway formed part of this road.

In the centuries after the Romans departed, England was gradually divided into Saxon kingdoms. Henbury became part of the kingdom of Mercia. In the pamphlet, *St Mary's Church Henbury – A Brief History*, it is explained that the known origins of Henbury Parish started when, "by a Charter of A.D. 692 King Ethelred of Mercia granted land at Henbury and Aust to Oftor, Bishop of Worcester." (Ethelred had been newly converted to Christianity.)

For centuries, the Bishops of Worcester had a palace near the site of Blaise Castle. In 1779 some ruins still marked its old position. Its existence until the fourteenth century is definitely established: see W.I. *A Guide to Henbury*. It is supposed that the Bishops provided a church there for their tenants who would have formed a village round it. There would have been farms to feed the landowners, their institutions and retainers.

It is possible to visualise a thriving community in Henbury at that time. As well as farmers, farm workers, toolmakers and smiths, there would also have been thatchers, woodsmen, potters, bakers, cooks and servants of all descriptions. Then there were clergy, scholars, and, for the many children (boys), there may well have been a choir school. No doubt there were markets, horse-fairs, religious festivals. Perhaps some of the crafts people kept shops.

A Brief History informs the reader that a charter in 1093 makes it clear that by that time, a church *had* been established at Henbury. There was also a chapel dedicated to St. Werburgh, the Mercian nun-princess who was a niece of King Ethelred. The chapel is thought to have been built on the old hill-fort. It is supposed that later a chapel to St. Blaise, patron saint of wool-carders, was erected here. Later again, the site was used for Blaise Castle.

Until a few years ago, the ancient Parish extended from Sea Mills to Aust, with three other churches or chapels at Aust, Northwick and Lawrence Weston. In the last hundred years or so, other churches have been established at Hallen, Sea Mills and Brentry. The modern parish now includes only Henbury, Brentry and Hallen. (*A Brief History*, 1970)

Norman Era

It seems that Henbury was an established community by the time of the Norman Conquest in A.D. 1066. Henbury became the manor of Henbury, and remained within church ownership until the sixteenth century.

The Normans replaced the Saxon kingdoms with their own method of organisation, the Feudal System. As Normans intermarried with Saxons, the people settled down, taking their ordered places in the 'system'. A strict hierarchy took hold of Norman England that demanded service and loyalty in exchange for protection and tenancies. All were included from the lowliest up through the lords, barons and finally to the monarch himself. In Henbury, authority and ownership were vested in the Bishops of Worcester.

The Feudal System brought stability to the country. Increased strictness and order enabled people to get on with their lives and work unhampered. It may be that some people looked back to earlier times when life was less organised and freer. Some overlords were known to have been harsh masters. Escape was difficult, but England was extensively wooded; malcontents could and did find a hiding place.

In the Norman era, many Saxon churches, some of stone, some constructed from mud and wattle, were gradually superseded by Norman-

Roman finds: fibula T-shaped brooch, found in Hallen Close field; bronze brooch, 1st/2nd century AD and coin found by Hallen Close

Medieval: silver ring brooch worn at the throat for fastening the undergarment; lead pilgrim's ampulla; brass belt hook, for hanging purse.

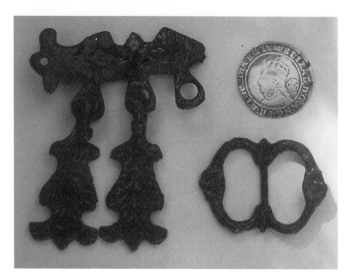

Tudor: sword belt fitment 1550–1600; Elizabethan silver sixpence, 1594; brass belt buckle, Tudor Rose design.

Stuart: silver double hoop spur buckle; James I silver shilling found behind Westmoreland Farmhouse, and worth more than a week's wage for a farm labourer; Charles I silver shilling, 1643.

Georgian: bronze tamper, for pressing tobacco in pipe bowl; 1806 halfpenny; watch key, copper alloy gilded, hung from the fob chain; bronze toy cannon.

Victorian: silver fan brooch; lady's silver pocket watch; silver thimble.

style architecture. The new churches were notable for their rounded pillars and arches. *A Brief History* tells us that the bases of some of the great pillars in Henbury Church supporting the roof today are of that period. St. Mary's Henbury was extended and modified between the twelfth and nineteenth centuries, reflecting the changing styles and fortune of the times. By the thirteenth century, a vicarage had been built on the site of the present Vestry Hall.

Middle Ages

From various church registers and monuments, one gets some idea how natural disasters and political events affected the lives of Henbury villagers. Floods are mentioned, from the River Severn. Although taxes were levied to build temporary protection, it appears that the river had no permanent flood barriers to protect land and households.

From *A Brief History* a 'swift succession' of vicars in 1369 suggests that the Black Death took a heavy toll of clergy. Villagers too would have been affected by this deadly outbreak. In the days thought of as the 'Middle Ages', Henbury village, tucked away in the far south west of Gloucestershire and in rural separation from the newly emerging Bristol, probably escaped much of the political unrest that beset London and other large cities.

However, the Lords Spiritual and the Lords Temporal held a fine balance of power in the country; and much of the land was held by the bishops. In 1463, Bishop Carpenter established Henbury Parish's independence from the powerful Dean and College at Westbury. (Part of the collegiate buildings still stands in College Road, Westbury.) But there still followed in later years challenges for various dues by Westbury's deans.

A link with royalty is seen from the records. *A Brief History* gives tantalising snippets of information. The vicar in 1485 was also physician to Prince Arthur and Prince Henry (later King Henry VIII). The clergy was constantly vigilant against frivolity on Sundays and during service times. One vicar, John Barlo, in 1536 nearly got into trouble when he reprimanded Lady Ann Berkely for such behaviour – the Lords Temporal and Spiritual in conflict?

Henry VIII

Henry's reign began in 1509 and ended in 1547. The systematic dissolution of the monasteries and redistribution of church lands is well-known. In Henbury, the land in 1547 was granted to Sir Ralph Sadleir who had been Falconer to the king and his one-time favourite. As well as the Manor of Henbury, Sir Ralph received the Manor House (along with Westbury and other extensive lands). However, he retained his Hertford-shire home as his principal seat and leased out Henbury Manor and House.

It is interesting to note that at about the end of this century, the earliest parts of Westmoreland and Norton farmhouses were being built.

Seventeenth and Eighteenth Centuries

About a century after Henbury was put into the hands of Sir Ralph, his grandson, also Ralph, died without children, and the Sadleir line ended. However, grandson Ralph's sister was married to Sir Walter Aston of Tixal in Staffordshire. Their son and heir, also Walter, sold Henbury (and Westbury) including the patronage of the church to land dealers in 1675, Thomas Yate and Gregory Gearing. (Westbury College had been ruined in 1643 during the Civil War.)

Until this time, Henbury had remained under single ownership, first of the church and then of the Sadleirs and their heirs. Farmers tilled the land as tenants, houses were built on land belonging to the owner. The influence of the Feudal System still pervaded in the power of landowners over tenure and employment.

In 1680, the land dealers sold the Manor and Hundred of Henbury, including the Manor House, to Sir Samuel Astry whose father-in-law, G. Morse had in 1665 built the original Great House on a piece of ground bought from the Sadleir family. Sir Samuel enlarged the house and, in creating a landscape for it, he planted an avenue of trees leading to a summer house on Blaise hill. When Astry purchased his land, there were a few 'excepted' plots including a field in Charlton sold to Mr Sampson, and lands in possession of Widow Norton and Richard Lott. In fact,

Astry also bought the Manors of Westbury on Trym (but not the college) and Stoke Bishop. All these manors extended far further than the present-day parishes.

This ownership was short lived. After Astry's death in 1704, his widow married Sir Simon Harcourt who had further work done on the house. Astry left no male heir. By 1715, his estates were divided between his three daughters, Elizabeth married to Sir James Smyth, Diana married to Richard Orlebar and Arabella married to Charles William, Earl of Suffolk. (Scipio Africanus, who died in 1720 aged 18, was their servant.)

Arabella and Charles lived at the Great House until their death in 1721. Ownership of Henbury was broken up further, and the house was sold separately. From this time on, there was further fragmentation of the land between family heirs.

Once the land had left the Sadleir family in the late seventeenth century, it was not long before successful Bristol merchants started to rent or buy land plots and build grand houses for themselves. This was the era of overseas trade including slaves and tobacco. The city was growing large and prosperous; merchants started looking for 'a place in the country'. One of the first of these was John Sampson of Charlton, who bought a plot of land near the church. By 1688, he had built an impressive gabled house on the foundations of an old residence, Awdelett House. He named his new house 'Henbury Awdelett'.

After the death of the Earl and Countess of Suffolk, the Blaise Estate part of Henbury seems to have passed via one of the Countess's sisters to the Smyths of Ashton Court, who held it until 1760, after selling the house in 1730.

In 1762, Thomas Farr bought the Blaise Estate and lived in the old manor house. In 1766 he demolished the summer house and erected the 'sham' castle on the hill. He was declared bankrupt in 1778, and the estate passed to Denham Skeate, a lawyer, who sold it to J.S. Harford in 1789.

It was now known as the Blaise Castle Estate because of the sham castle. The Harford family kept the estate together over three generations until within the living memory of some older villagers. It was sold in 1926 to Bristol Corporation which, to everyone's relief, has kept it as a beautiful public park.

As regards the rest of Henbury, in Rudder's book, *A New History of Gloucester, 1779*, it seems that 'Ownership of Henbury was broken up between Smyths and part sold to E. Colston and heirs. By 1775 it

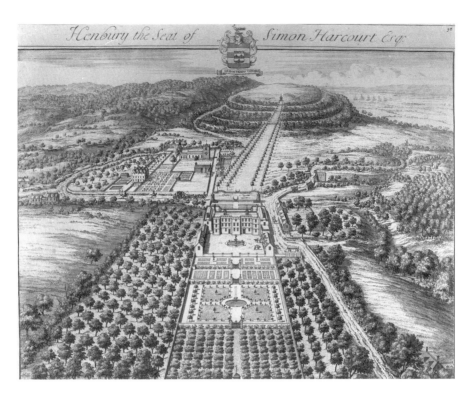

The Great House and Sir Samuel Astry's park. Engraving by Johannes Kip, 1712. [City of Bristol Museums and Art Gallery]

The Old Manor House, Henbury. [British School drawing, City of Bristol Museums and Art Gallery]

belonged to Francis Lord Middleton and Colston. In 1779, Sir Jarret Smith was the owner of one moity; and the Hon. Thomas Willoughby, second son of Lord Middleton, and Alex Colston were proprietors of the other moity.' These owners seem to have kept Henbury village intact, although selling plots lining Henbury Road and Hallen Road for limited private building.

Nineteenth Century

Ownership of the two larger farms, Westmoreland and Norton, changed. The tithing map of 1839 and Henbury Rates Book show that Edward Sampson was then the owner, his family having purchased the land some time in the previous sixty years. They remained in the possession of the Sampson-Way family until the compulsory purchase order in 1947.

Maybe Henbury retained its rural character so long by virtue of the rise of wealthy merchants who valued beautiful homes in rural retreat while there were also 'custodians' who wished to preserve farming as a way of life. This was sometimes also a lucrative enterprise and a status symbol for the owner.

From the days of the neolithic farmers, Henbury dwellings have come and gone. From the late sixteenth century onwards, farm steads, a number of cottages and small houses as well as some large handsome houses have been preserved.

A villager remarked, 'The surviving "old Henbury" houses are mostly "posh" these days. Where did the workers live?' What *did* happen to the many houses occupied by ordinary families down the centuries? Apart from the church, no building from before about the 1580s has survived. From research into other villages, it seems that it was usual in the Middle Ages and later for church, manor house and sometimes vicarage to be constructed of stone, while ordinary dwellings were timber-framed, filled in between with rubble/clay under a thatched roof. In time, these fell into ruin or were demolished to be replaced when and where needed. Small stone houses that superseded them were often later extended and 'gentrified'.

But in fact it was not just the humble cottage that was destroyed. In Henbury the Manor House described in *A Popular Retreat* as 'essentially a seventeenth century structure, may have incorporated a mediaeval building', was pulled down and replaced by Blaise Castle House. The Great House too was demolished by Thomas Stock who replaced it with Henbury Court. In its turn, this last house came down in about 1953 for new schools and housing.

Henbury Village. [from the
collection of Bygone Bristol]

Henbury village stores in 1950.

4 – The Village Street

Some of the shops in the village street were housed in buildings dating far back in antiquity, but villagers in the early twentieth century were, of course, concerned only with the services they had to offer. Looking back now, they are aware of tremendous changes during their life-span; from uncomplicated rural life-style to an existence dominated by high-tech. Life in the 1990s is in general more comfortable than eighty years ago, yet there remains nostalgia for the way things used to be.

Near church and close was that part of Henbury Road that contained the village shops and trades. Together with church and school, it formed the centre of village life. With virtually no public transport, unless one possessed a horse or bike, one walked. Businesses, though few, were essential to a rural community. On one side of the road was the blacksmith's shop and the Post Office. Across the road was the Clerk to the Magistrates Court, then the sweet shop and cobbler's. Next came the Porter Stores, Rossiter the Undertaker, the village shop and the plumber and taxi service.

Clothing had changed little since late Victorian times. Women wore long dresses, long hair piled on top of their heads and covered with enormous hats. Children's clothes were of heavy fabrics meant to last, and they wore iron-tipped boots. After the war, dress styles started to change. In the forefront were the 'flappers' who introduced short skirts and 'bobbed' hair. Older women took longer to accept this dramatic change. Women walked round the village carrying large shopping baskets. The village shop held only basic groceries so some mothers would take their baskets over the hill to Westbury. The two-hourly bus service, afternoons only, meant that they usually walked, one way at least. Other families relied on Westbury grocers and their horse-drawn vans to deliver a weekly order to the door.

Freedom from traffic in the village street meant that people walked on the road as well as the pavement. Children would bowl their hoops along the road as they made for the sweetshop. Mothers would gather together there before walking along Station Road to collect their small children from school. The baker's cobern regularly passed through the street at a leisurely pace, the horse-bus might be seen or a coal cart pulled by huge drays. Biggs Dairy carts made deliveries twice daily. People, horses, delivery drivers, all shared the road with plenty of time to give way to each other. An impressive sight before Mrs Harford's death in 1919 was her coachman Mr Tom George driving her carriage and pair through Blaise Castle House gates.

What sounds struck the ear? The villagers could hear the jingle of horses' harness, hammer on anvil, people's voices, animal voices, birdsong, children's laughter. And the smells? Woodsmoke was pervasive, muck spread on fields, droppings on the road from cows, sheep, horses; perhaps a whiff of cesspit! But just humans and animals; no engine noise or exhaust fumes.

Many of the women returned to their houses to boil their washing without running water; to brush and beat carpets without sweepers or vacuum cleaners. They had to carry coals to their cooking ranges, and clear out the ashes. They had to ladle water into a tin bath by the boiler – no bathroom! They needed to light candles and oil lamps when it got dark. Village women could not afford domestic help. They themselves and their daughters would at some time seek domestic work in the grand Henbury houses.

Henbury Post Office

"In 1778, Mr Thomas Farr became bankrupt and sold the Blaise Castle Estate, Inn and Blacksmith's Shop to Denham Skeate, a lawyer who shortly after, sold them to Mr J S Harford."

In 1984, Mr R Govier transcribed the memoirs of Mr Maurice Stevens and deposited them in Blaise Castle House museum. As they throw a great deal of light on the history of this part of the village, extracts from them will be widely used.

"My great grandfather, John Warburton had his grocer's shop and Post Office among a group of cottages between the wall bordering the road opposite the Hallen turning and the high wall bordering Blaise lawn. They were demolished about 1890–93. My father, Joseph was born there. I came across the wall when I was a boy, and also traces of limework on the high wall underneath the ivy.

"To replace these cottages, Mr Harford built two new houses outside the Blaise entrance on the site of the demolished Castle Inn. One [was]

32

Henbury Post Office, c.1880.

for John Warburton to carry on his business, and the other for Mr Jarrett, the farm bailiff and his wife who attended to the dairy in the garden, £1 per week was their combined wage. An extra room was added to the post office to enable Mrs Warburton to continue supplying refreshment to any travellers happening to visit the village. Drinking water was piped up to these two houses as well as to the Mansion from the spring in the lower pond in the woods."

Mr Stevens talked about the old Castle Inn, the original old pub, in Henbury 'village street':

"The Castle Inn stood on the site of the present Post Office and Corner House. It was demolished prior to 1880, as this was about the date that my great grandfather moved to the new Post Office from his cottage shop. The foundations of the old Inn were discovered some distance from the present boundary wall, making the road narrower on the corner than it is today. The only remaining part of the Inn today is the building behind the Post Office, now used as a hairdressers. This was the stable belonging to the Inn and my father kept his fowls there before the building was converted by Mr Harford into a village club room. A Mr Prewitt was the carpenter involved. The present door of this building is the original front door of the old Inn and has a massive lock attached which, unfortunately, has disappeared recently. I have the door handle and the huge key which once belonged to the lock. The cellars of the Inn must have contained rainwater. It was drawn up by pumps placed in the scullery of the two houses. Access to this, I understand, can be obtained underneath the hearthstone in the Post Office. The only reference to the old Inn that I have come across is that a dinner was given there by Mr Harford to seventy men to celebrate the roofing of the new Mansion, and each man was given a gallon of ale."

According to the Census of 1891, John Warburton, by that time aged eighty one and retired as sub-postmaster, had been living for about ten years at the new Post Office with his wife, Mary and their daughter Sarah Stevens who was then sub-postmistress. Also living there were Sarah's children: Edith aged twenty one and assistant postmistress, sixteen-year-old Joseph who was rural postman, and Margaret, still at school.

Maurice wrote that his father, Joseph, married at the age of twenty four. He and his wife had two children, Maurice and Marjorie. Joseph continued as postman until retirement and his sister Margaret was sub-postmistress from 1909 until her retirement. After the Harford family vacated Blaise Castle Estate in 1926, The Corner House came up for sale and in 1927 Joseph bought it for £400. Descendants of John Warburton continued to live next door to each other for many years after this, as eventually Marjorie took over from her Aunt Margaret, and brought her family to live at the Post Office.

Marjorie had married Charles Hellen; David is their son. Her brother Maurice had a son and a daughter, Pauline. She says that when her grandfather, Joseph retired in December 1935, the local inhabitants made him a presentation to express "our sincere appreciation of the unfailing courtesy and kindness we have received from you during the many years you have acted as our postman".

Joseph also owned the café attached to his house. David Hellen believes he started this after retirement. This café building (now a house) is thought to have been originally the 'Reading Room' or 'club' referred to by Maurice. David has written:

"The café was very busy, and I can still see Grandad in the kitchen slicing bread, and warming the butter in front of the range. I imagine that bread, butter and jam and a pot of tea was all that was served for tea. But he sold something else also. The Miss Perretts of Beaconsfield would make up bunches of flowers from their garden for Grandad to sell in the café."

Families coming for outings to the recently opened Blaise Estate must have found Joseph's café very welcome.

David goes on to describe his memories of living at the Post Office:

"When we moved to the Post Office in 1943, when mother became sub-postmistress, we still had a pump in the 'back kitchen'. There was also company's water of course, but we used the pump for baths. I was told that when the two houses were built . . . the cellars of the Inn were not filled in, but were turned into a cistern for rainwater that ran off the roofs of the two houses. I never knew exactly where this was, and as far as I know, it never had to be opened up, but it supplied the two houses and never ran dry. The cast iron pumps have been long since removed but I imagine that the cistern is still there! There was a copper in the corner of the back kitchen but I can't remember it ever being used and it must have soon been taken out. I think that we used to heat up the water for baths in a gas-fired copper, and this was poured into a tin bath until we had an Ascot heater and a fixed bath installed. We had no garden, just a yard with a coalhouse and outside toilet, but it did have a flush!"

David remembers that his mother sold newspapers when she took over from her aunt Margaret Stevens. He writes:

"I would be woken up in the mornings (except Sundays) by the sound of the W.H. Smith driver throwing the bundles into the porch. (The large outer door to the porch was a later addition.) This thump was followed half a minute later by the crash as the Corporation sawyer opened the double doors into the nursery so as he could get into the sawmill the back way. He, the sawyer had this arrangement with the W.H. Smith driver to have a lift every day.

"The doors were secured(?) by a baulk of timber resting in slots across the inside, and it was a simple matter for him to slip his hand between the wall and the door and give the plank a flip. He was a large man and we all called him 'giant'. I believe his name was Mr Harvey, and his assistant was Mr Pullin from Ison Hill. The sawmill itself was through the lower set of double doors nearer Telephone Cottage. He was a good friend to Granny (Jo's wife) especially after Grandad died in 1946, and kept her supplied with 'chumps' – off-cuts for her fire.

"The evening papers were a different arrangement. Mr Pollard, who lived in the Hamlet, did a paper round: he collected them from Kingsweston Park gate every afternoon. He would then deliver his papers and drop our small bundle when he got back to Henbury."

The Forge

Essential to an agricultural community was the blacksmith. Mr Parmenas J Grigg shod horses and repaired farm machinery and other metal goods. Every small village needed the services of a smithy when horse power meant just that. Mr Grigg's son, also 'Jimmy', had his own smithy in nearby Westbury. P J Grigg lived in a tall old house beside his shop where horses were led from the street through the door to the forge. These buildings almost certainly date from at least the seventeenth century.

Sometimes farmers would employ a farrier who visited the farm to shoe horses taking with him a portable anvil. Farriers also became proficient in dealing with minor equine ailments.

The heat of the village forge, glare of the coals, hammering and shaping, the flying sparks were a fascinating experience for the young village boys. It is all well-remembered by contributors to this book.

After P J Grigg's retirement and in the early 1940s his house and shop became 'Holly House'. *Kelly's Directory* lists Mrs Eliza Webber living at Holly

Mail cart behind Porter Stores.

Farrier at Norton Farm, 1956.

House at that time, but by 1944 Mrs Eve Hitchings is listed as having a shop there until it was taken over by the Brown family after the war.

David remembers the days of Mrs Brown as shopkeeper. "It was," he says, "the most general of general stores and sold pretty well everything – sweets, paraffin, cigarettes, groceries, newspapers etc. The shop where you actually went to make a purchase was the front room: in the front door, up the hall, turn right. But the stock was everywhere! The building adjoining, lower down the hill (at one time the forge) was full of goods, some of it displayed in the window, but in a terrible jumble."

David thinks that Mrs Brown died in the mid to late 1940s. "Then her son, Tom Brown took on the business (he also ran a garage at Pilning) but did not live in Holly House. (Tom was the famous England rugby full-back who, having been approached by a Rugby League team was banned from the Union game for life. He has only recently been posthumously exonerated!) He must have sold the shop for he went on to become the Landlord of the White Hart at Olveston.

"The next owners of Holly House were the Edwards family from Hallen Road. They used the house as a house, turning the old forge into a shop."

Across the street and a little lower down was Mr Charles Newman's house, Raglan Villa.

Charles Newman came to Henbury as a very young man from his native Devon. His own father a schoolmaster, Charles's first job was as assistant master at the Boys' School just about the time it ceased to be the Anthony Edmonds School (about 1890s), for a few of the older boys were 'Blue Boys' when he arrived.

Later, he became Clerk to the Magistrates Court in Hallen Road. He had a small office built at the side of his house from where he conducted these duties and his other business interests including tax collection and administration of various trusts and charities. He was knowledgeable, and villagers would seek his advice on many matters.

Charles married a Henbury girl and they had three daughters and a son. In the early days they owned a small back garden. Later, perhaps in the 1920s, Charles bought a large garden, orchard and land behind his house (now part of Battersby Way). His wife died when their son Percy was a baby. Percy was cared for by his sisters who tried to compensate for his grief and their own. In due time, he married and had a family. He joined the R.A.F. in the Second World War and was killed when his aircraft was shot down.

Many villagers grieved with the family at the loss of this interesting and personable young man. He was deprived of his mother in babyhood; so also were his two young daughters deprived of their father in early childhood.

Mr and Mrs William Windsor's shop

Next to Raglan Villa, Mrs Maisie Windsor kept a sweetshop, and in the room behind the shop her husband plied his craft of 'cobbling'. The sweetshop was popular, especially with the children, with its shiny brass scales and rows of glass jars full of boiled sweets of every shape, flavour and colour. In exchange for one penny, a halfpenny or even one farthing, they could purchase some of these delightful goodies.

The room behind was a hive of industry. Work on farms, and miles of daily walking bore heavily on footwear and this was where farmers and villagers brought hobnailed boots and other heavy shoes and boots of every kind.

The Porter Stores

A dictionary definition of 'porter': "Historically, porter was a dark brown bitter beer brewed from charred or browned malt, originally made especially for porters. A local pub landlord defines porter as Stout".

For many years, porter was retailed at the Porter Stores in Henbury village street. The house is largely eighteenth century probably with seventeenth century origins (Henbury Conservation leaflet, 1987). Villagers remember that there were wooden benches round the back and in the yard. Reginald Townsend was the proprietor in the 1940s and by 1950 it was Stanley Rudman. In the late 1950s, it became Blaise Inn with a full licence and incorporated the Windsors' old shop, turning it into a lounge bar.

In the early twentieth century, the mail cart would drive into the Porter Stores yard to await deliveries and collections at the Post Office opposite.

Undertaker

Next to the Porter Stores stood some old cottages. In the garden behind them Rossiter the undertaker had a workshop and yard where he kept his materials and made up the coffins. Some villagers recall that he also had a timber yard on the corner of Hallen Road opposite the Police Station.

Village Stores

Ray recalls that, shortly after the Great War, the cottage in front of Rossiters was a private house. The householder rented out a front room to Westminster Bank so that a sub-branch could be held there between 1 and 2 pm on weekdays. Mr H W. Giles was manager in about 1930.

Later after the bank closed, a village store was opened. According to the *Street Directory*, in 1944 Mr Fred Hudson was keeping shop. Memories agree he was managing the shop for Mr K Lynch who was away at the war. The 1947 directory shows Mr Lynch back in charge. Later on Mrs Tincknell ran the shop.

The Village Stores was a general shop, most useful for day-to-day needs of every description.

Plumber and Taxi Service

Herbert Harvey and his family lived in the cottage next to the village stores. All the village knew Mr Harvey who was the local plumber, decorator etc and at one time also the village taxi service.

As a young man Ray was a close friend of Arthur, one of the Harvey sons. Ray and Arthur took part in numerous skittles and darts matches between the wars.

David writes: "The Harveys' house itself appears to be very old but the real magnificence of the property was his workshop (just where the new house stands). It was a treasury of all the bits and pieces left over from jobs, saved 'because you never know what might come in useful!'"

Houses in the Village Street

Further down the hill from the smithy are two houses, Hillside and Beaconsfield. Opposite is Alma Villa, semi-detached to Raglan Villa.

Hillside is a small, most attractive cottage built in the early nineteenth century. It was then owned by the Sampson-Way family, and used to house an employee and his family. The last of such occupants that villagers remember was a Mrs Miller, thought to be the widow of George Miller, listed in *Kelly's Directory* as 'woodman'. In her old age, it is said that Mrs Miller became a little eccentric and some of the children were afraid of her.

In 1951, after the Sampson-Way estates were dispersed Hillside was sold, the first private owner being Mrs E D Hall. The cottage then passed between several owners until, in 1983, it was purchased by the present 'incumbent', Mrs E M Day. Mrs Day is happily placed because her daughter, Susan and grandchildren live next door. Their house was once P J Grigg's house and blacksmith shop.

Beaconsfield, an unusual and beautiful single-story house was built around 1923, when Mrs Perrett, a widow, and her adult daughters left their home in Wotton-under-Edge to live in Henbury. Mrs Perrett commissioned an architect who had designed houses for hotter climes, and this is reflected in the style of Beaconsfield. The roofs slope down over broad eaves. There are arches and cornices. Corridors leave the hallway at interesting angles. The house is enclosed within a secret garden of lawns and shrubs. A path winds up from the road and all is protected by a high stone wall.

The present owner, Mrs Pat Jacob says that the house was on the site of the orchard belonging to Henbury Awdelett and that planning permission was conditional on its being single-storied probably because the Sampson-Way family did not want their view obstructed. A map of 1881 seems to indicate that this site was once part of the avenue of trees planted by Sir Samuel Astry between his Great House (corner of Station Road) and the small summer house at the top of Blaise Hill (before the castle was built).

There were two Miss Perretts and a married sister, Mrs Keel (a London-trained nurse and midwife). They are all remembered as very keen gardeners. Besides keeping their large garden in beautiful order, they made wine, sweets and their own Christmas cards and calendars.

David remembers that another of their interests was stamp-collecting. They passed on to him an old Stanley Gibbons Catalogue. Their charitable works included collecting for 'Waifs and Strays' now called The Children's Society.

In 1966 the last of the Perrett sisters died, and Mrs Jacob, their cousin's daughter, inherited the house. So Beaconsfield has been kept within the family since its beginning.

Alma Villa Across the road stands Alma Villa semi-detached with Raglan Villa. For many years Alma Villa was the home of Mr R A Edwards and family.

The Hollies, Woodlands and Rosebank

Beyond Henry Harvey's house and workshop are three large residences. 'The Hollies' stands alone, 'White Lodge' (until the 1950s called 'Woodlands') and 'Rose Bank' are semi-detached. Painted white with low-pitched roofs and sash windows, they stand solid and handsome in the style much used in the eighteenth century. In an account of her house 'The Hollies', Mrs A Claxton writes:

"The house has features that suggest it was originally far smaller, and has been built onto and 'gentrified'. It has two roofs. We think the rear roof, clad in ordinary terracotta clay pantiles covers the extent of the original house. Here, the rooms are fairly small with low ceilings. There is a beautiful old stone and wood fireplace in the kitchen with an old wooden cupboard to one side. The two bedrooms in this part of the house still have old iron fireplaces. Between this part of the house and the front, there are very thick walls, probably the original exterior ones.

"The front part of the house is much more elegant and up market. The roof facing the road is of expensive slate whereas the back of the front roof is like the rear roof i.e. pantiles. The rooms are larger here, have higher ceilings, pretty arches and cornices. The two downstairs rooms now have eighteenth century marble fireplaces found in a junk shop in Bristol. We hope they resemble the originals that were missing when we purchased the house. The hall is very pretty with an elegant curved staircase bannister dating from the eighteenth century.

"The house was also built onto early this century – a porch/ conservatory was added at the back and a large room added to the side.

There had also been a large room at the back recently demolished to make a terrace.

"We think the house in its original form features in the Kip engravings of the area. Certainly it must date from seventeenth century or earlier. The hand-made eighteenth century wooden front porch (under a canopy) contains 120 mortice and tenon joints.

"We were told by the previous owners that it had been a farmhouse and that the land belonging to it had extended past Henbury Comprehensive School. [Perhaps this was land farmed later by Arthur Hawkins.] We were also informed that the upstairs windows at the front are of a construction that dates them around 1727."

The Claxtons bought 'The Hollies' from the Silvey family. Earlier, Mrs Wellington lived there.

White Lodge and Rose Bank: In the Henbury Conservation Society leaflet, one reads that these two houses are contemporary with the Hamlet (completed 1811) and were also built by Harford: "The strong vertical lines and delicate glazing bars of these Regency houses were preceded in architectural fashion by the horizontal emphasis and much heavier glazing bars to be seen in their neighbour 'The Hollies'."

However, Mr Venables the owner of 'Rose Bank', points out that window features in his house indicate an earlier date – possibly eighteenth century – another case of 'alteration, extension and gentrification', perhaps?

Miss A Baker lived for many years at 'The Woodlands' (later named 'White Lodge'). We are also told that at one time, it was purchased by the then Vicar of Henbury for the use of his curate. This is likely to have been in the incumbency of one of the Way family. Behind the village street there are two houses opening onto Church Lane, 'Applegarth' and 'Telephone Cottage'.

Applegarth

After Astry land was sold off in 1760, some of it was bought by the Sampson-Way family. The 'avenue' was then gradually demolished as the land was needed for other purposes. We understand that 'Applegarth' was built originally as a single storied stone cottage to house a Sampson-Way employee.

The Hollies.

Telephone Cottage.

David recalls that as a small boy he would sit on a chair outside the back door of the house having his hair cut by Mr Simmonds for 6d.

There was a tragic incident connected with the house in the 1960s when Mr and Mrs Locke lived there. Their only daughter was murdered in Blaise woods while walking her dog.

Telephone Cottage

This is at the other end of Church Lane from Applegarth. It stands right on the lane and is made of grey stone with a door between two bow windows. On the door is written, 'Telephone Cottage'.

Old documents show that in 1707 the land on which it was built belonged to the Anthony Edmonds Trust and was leased to the Harcourt/Astry family for an annual rent of ten shillings.

By 1799 there was a 'messuage, cottage or tenement' erected on the land by Francis Henry Brooke. Various occupiers are named over succeeding years as the house was sold on; Miss Clara Baker lived there from 1936 until 1944, in 1954, Mrs Short is known to have been in occupation. She remained there until 1974 when Mrs Joyce Steele, the present owner bought the house. (we were told that Mr Short was valet to the then Speaker of the House of Commons.)

Mrs Steele discovered how her house came by its name: It was amongst the earliest to possess a telephone and the very first in Henbury. In 1877/78, the house was used as part of a system of 'Call Offices' to which messages could be taken to be transmitted and then delivered by messenger. A telegraph pole sited opposite (in the garden where 'Beaconsfield' was later built) brought in an annual rent for the owner of the garden.

Villagers remember that the Call Office was used by the Harfords of Blaise Castle House. Some people recall that it later became the village's public telephone when entry was through a door on the right hand side of the front door. This 'entry' is now replaced by a bow window.

The Vicarage from the yard, 1887.

46

5 – Three Mansions close to the Church

The Vicarage

In the *WI Guide to Henbury*, one reads that there are records of a thirteenth century vicarage, "on a site north of the church where the Vestry hall stands today. It had a courtyard, a garden, a croft (ie a meadow) called 'Elmehay' next to the garden and beyond that, a wood." The church at that time would have been Norman in style and smaller than it is today.

Chapter 3 mentions Henbury clergy, some of whom would have lived in the early vicarage. William Vance was vicar in Henbury when Bishop Carpenter examined the endowment of the vicarage in 1463. In 1574 Vicar John Northbrook "published a treatise against dancing, dicing and vayne plays on the Sabbath." (Extracts from *A Brief History*.)

John Gardiner (1729–79) must have been a fairly early occupant of the new vicarage which was built 1729. Walter Trevelyan, the well-known naturalist was vicar during the nineteenth century, immediately before Henry Hugh Way took over in 1830. He was followed by his son John Hugh Way in 1860, and then his grandson C P Way, in 1906.

The vicarage was built with gardens overlooking the Dell and the Hazel Brook. The Way family was well-connected and 'monied'. During their hundred years of occupation, the vicarage was extended by the addition of bedrooms and kitchens suited to the way of life of a wealthy family, employing a large domestic staff. To deflect a right of way crossing their garden they had a tunnel constructed that led from the Royalls to the churchyard.

At the end of this clerical 'dynasty' in 1928, such a vicarage was quite inappropriate to the life-style of a modern clergy family. A new vicarage was then built in Station Road near to the Girls' and Infants' School. The old clergy house was sold to Dr W K Wills who remained there with his family for at least twenty years until the 1950s. Since they left, other families have owned the house and in the 1990s, it is the home of Mr and Mrs T Parkinson.

Peter explained how he came to live in the vicarage, albeit for only a short time. He has a special attachment to the house because he was

The Steep Path, Henbury Vicarage.

Family portrait, 1887.

48

The Vicarage Steps.

born there! His father, Francis was employed by Dr Wills as chauffeur. When the doctor had moved into the house in about 1928, he brought with him, as well as his own family, Frank, his wife, a son and two daughters. He gave Francis and his family the garden flat to live in.

After their second son Peter was born, Dr Wills invited the family to take occupation of another property he owned, number 2 Elm Cottages. When the new baby was about 12 months old, they moved to their more spacious accommodation. The garden flat was then occupied by Edwin Bailey and his wife. Mr Bailey was Dr Wills' gardener.

Canon John Collins Lloyd became vicar after the Rev. C P Way and, with his family, was the first to live in the twentieth century 'new' vicarage. Robert Biggs remembers playing cricket on the new vicarage lawn with the vicar's son, a boy about his own age.

One of the villagers recalls that, "Dr Kenneth Wills was a retired medical man who had specialised", he was told, "in skin complaints." He continued, "Mrs Wills was one of the local ladies who were rather 'looked up to'. There were others, Mrs Gunn, Mrs Chetwood-Aiken (of Berwick Lodge), Mrs Blandy and Mrs Thornton-Wood who all had the same 'aura' – tweeds, grey hair, good speakers, enthusiastic manner. I don't think that they looked down at the villagers but we tended to respect them. My Granny would have called them 'gentry'. Any of the village events would have had a little extra added to it if any of them were present. I suppose today, they would be classed as 'do-gooders' but I think that they were necessary to village life at that time. I expect that they considered that they had certain 'responsibilities' to the affairs of the village. Mrs Kenneth Wills for instance would often hold fund-raising affairs in the billiard room at the top of the stable-yard just opposite the front door of her house. Sales of work, that sort of thing. And I think the WI and/or Mothers' Union would meet there."

Henbury Awdelett (known as Henbury Manor)

Several villagers have visited the house, for example farmers Ray and Tom as tenants of the Sampson-Way family. "Each year," said Farmer Ray, "we went up to the Major's house at the annual rent audit. Here, with other farmers we were served a glass of sherry while we waited in turn to discuss repairs and other matters with the major." Tom added, "Yes, it was the major in our farming days, but my father and Ray's grandfather would see the old General who was the Major's father. When General Sampson-Way became elderly, he went to live at Berwick Lodge, north of the railway track, leaving his son, the Major with his family in occupation of Henbury Awdelett."

Peter's memory of the interior of the house was during the war. It appears that their Anderson air-raid shelter became water-logged and the Major, who at the time was Henbury's chief air-raid warden, heard of their plight. In Peter's words, "During the 'blitz' in 1940, the Major came to our rescue and invited the family to shelter in his cellars during the raids so we took down camp beds, deck chairs, sandwiches, thermos flasks etc; and were dry and safe. There was only one snag, however: to get to the lavatories, you had to pass Blotto, the dog, who vociferously guarded the dining room door!"

Henbury Awdelett, also known as the Manor House.

If you stand on the 'Showground' and look over the stone wall before the trees are in leaf, you can get a good view of Henbury Awdelett. It has been greatly extended over the years, and is an impressive sight. In more recent times, it became known as 'Henbury Manor' though it was never a manor house. (The Manor House had stood for centuries on the site now occupied by Blaise Dairy.)

It seems that Henbury Awdelett was probably the first of the grand houses (still surviving) to be built in the village; and was certainly the longest to endure with the original family. In the seventeenth century, John Sampson of Charlton had bought a plot of land near the church. On the plot were foundations of an earlier building, known as Awdelett House. By 1688, Mr Sampson had built his house and called it 'Henbury Awdelett'. In a later century, additions were made by his descendants who continued to live there until about 1950, when Bristol City Council bought it, and it became a school.

Since 1688, the family bought land in and beyond Henbury Village. Within the span of their residence, the Great House was pulled down, Blaise Castle House built in 1795 was finally abandoned by its family in 1926; Henbury Court was built 1807, demolished 1953. And here Henbury Awdelett still stands a lasting memorial to John Sampson's family.

During the mid-nineteenth century, the family name became Sampson-Way. The story of the Sampsons and the Ways is of some interest. In the 1830s, Edward Sampson, great great grandson of John Sampson of Charlton married Belinda Way, daughter of Colonel Ben Way and Mary (Smyth) Way. In 1831, Henry Hugh Way had succeeded Walter Trevelyan as Vicar of St. Mary's Church, Henbury. It is possible that Belinda Way, sister to Henry Hugh Way, met Edward on a visit to her brother. They fell in love and married. When their first son was born in 1838, they named him Nowell FitzUpton 'Sampson-Way'. Ever since then, the family has continued to be known by that name. The baby Nowell grew up to be the General to whom Farmers Tom and Ray's predecessors paid their rent. The General died in 1926.

One can imagine a close friendship between the Henbury Awdelett and Vicarage families. For three generations, the Way family provided vicars for St. Mary's living at the vicarage for nearly one hundred years. There is a door in the Sampson-Ways' wall just below the four steps leading to the east end of the church This door is close to the vicarage gate where probably the children and their families visited each other informally by this quick access. This close family connection could provide a clue to the renaming of Henbury Awdelett as Henbury Manor.

After the break up of Sadleir land in Henbury some of it went, via Sir Samuel Astry, into the Smyth family. Perhaps Belinda's mother, a Smyth, had an interest in the Lordship of the Manor of Henbury?

Blaise Castle House

This fine eighteenth-century house, sited not very far from the west end of the churchyard, is rectangular in shape, and has a circular pillared portico and sizeable conservatory. Still in place are some of the stone balustrades and classical inspired urns. The house lies near to the village end of the Estate. Just inside the gate leading to the village stands the stable block designed by William Paty.

The house was also the work of Paty who designed it as a family home for John Scandrett Harford, a Quaker banker. It was completed about 1795 to replace the old Henbury Manor house that had stood where John Nash later built the dairy. J S Harford then had the Estate landscaped by Humphrey Repton, including the scenic drive from the Lodge at the top of Henbury hill (designed to complement the castle), passing a woodsman's cottage to arrive at the house. In 1806 John Nash designed the conservatory.

Three generations of Harfords kept the house and estate going: J S, his son, also J S and a grandson, John Battersby Harford. As well as their woods and parkland (approximately 191 acres) they owned land in the village including part of the village street, and farmland on the Henbury side of Westbury. (Lampeter and Falcondale Roads were named after J B Harford's Estate in South Wales.)

Their employees must have accounted for a sizeable portion of the village population, for as well as a large domestic staff there were estate workers, and gardeners, grooms, coachman etc. In 1919, this Henbury dynasty came to an end with the death of Austrian-born Mary Harford, who was said to have been 'Presented' at the court of the German Kaiser. By 1926 all the property except the Hamlet had been sold to Bristol Council.

From then on, Blaise Castle Estate was opened up as a charming pleasure ground. Children could go in and climb the trees, fish in the stream, play games on the parkland. Families went there for picnics and walks.

The Harfords had pastured their cattle and sheep on the park, the ha-ha had kept the animals well away from the house. For some time after

Blaise Castle House and Blaise Hamlet

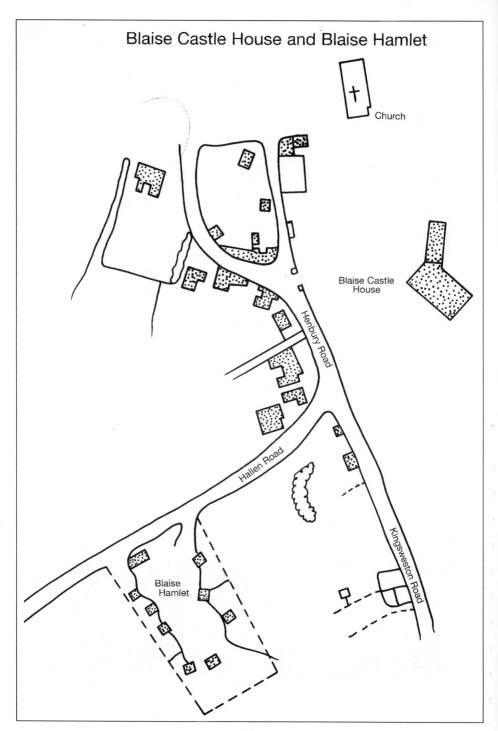

Church

Blaise Castle House

Henbury Road

Hallen Road

Kingsweston Road

Blaise Hamlet

From *The Red Book*: The Manor House and its successor, Blaise Castle House 'before and after', 1795. [City of Bristol Museums and Art Gallery]

Blaise Castle. [watercolour drawing by J.M. Field, 1827. City of Bristol Museums and Art Gallery.]

Blaise for the people: a young Paul Edmead walking in the park, 1958.

THE UPPER GATE, BLAISE CASTLE WOODS.

The Upper Gate, Blaise. [from the collection of Bygone Bristol]

the family left, local farmers kept their cattle there until eventually the ha-ha was levelled out and no more animals grazed after that.

From the memoirs of Mr Maurice Stevens, one learns that the sham gothic castle on the hill "was occupied by different people, at one time by Mr Davis, the woodman. To go to bed his son, Jack, climbed to the top of the tower and his bedroom was through a door into one of the side towers. I don't think that any water was laid on, so water for drinking was fetched from the Mansion. The stairs up to the tower, I remember, were polished and slippery. In the upper rooms cabinets of china and old armour were displayed My father made only one delivery of mail here each day, as it was considered a bit off the beaten track."

Mr Stevens also offered the following information:

"Thomas Farr had sold the Estate to Denham Skeate of Bath in 1788. In 1789 J S Harford made an offer of £11,000 for the Estate, also Blaise Inn (I think he meant 'Castle Inn') and the Blacksmith's shop. The

58

Mansion built in 1795 measured 66ft by 58ft without the long wing or picture room which were added in 1832."

Kings Weston Road

There were just a few houses along this road that were part of the village. None are ancient but some of their owners were part of village life. A villager offers the following:

"Along Kings Weston Road – Blaise Cottage, householder Mr Taylor. Then there was an allotment. Next comes Little Reynoldston, Mr Casson and later, Mr Brown. At Meadowbank, owned by National Smelting Co. Avonmouth and used by them for entertaining and the accommodation of visitors, Mr Hunter was the Caretaker/Caterer. Woodcroft was the home of Mr and Mrs Evans. Mrs Evans was an invalid and the house was built in chalet style for her comfort. At Cotswold House, built 1940 lived the Coventrys. Mr Coventry was part of Wilkins and Coventry, the Builders. Mrs Coventry was sister to Mrs Lynch at the Village Stores.

"Four Stacks was built post-war, owner Mr Evans i/c Vehicle Licensing. He later ran the Tea Gardens at New Passage. These Tea Gardens had been created by Mr Edwin Collins, a New Passage farmer who was grandfather to Farmer Ray McEwen Smith. Next door at Holdenhurst was Stuart Evans, Solicitor. He arranged for the old font at St. Mary's to be re-erected in the churchyard in memory of his wife. And at South Lodge were the Moores."

6 – Hallen Road

Police Station and Court

At the top of Hallen Road, just round the corner from 'Rose Bank', a handsome set of buildings, now used as private dwellings, had been built for use as Henbury's police station and courthouse. They date from 1906.

Kelly's Directory 1931 (Gloucestershire) ". . . county court district of Bristol, Lawford's Gate petty sessional division . . . A petty sessional court is held at Henbury on the first Tuesday in each month."

Everyone seems to remember Sgt. Harding who was the officer in charge of the station and court at Henbury. He kept a keen eye on village and villagers as he cycled round his 'beat'. Ray remembers being caught by the sergeant when, in his youth he was caught riding his motorcycle on the road without a licence. Such small crimes were dealt with at Henbury police court where Charles Newman was Clerk to the magistrates, who included among their number Major Sampson-Way of Henbury Awdelett and Mrs Budgett of Tramore.

A little way down Hallen Road and almost opposite the police station can be found one of Henbury's 'show' places, Blaise Hamlet.

Blaise Hamlet

In 1807 J S Harford, about twelve years after building his mansion, bought a piece of land across Kings Weston Road and commissioned John Nash to design a hamlet as a retreat for his old servants when they retired. The cottages were built between 1810 and 1812.

Maurice Stevens records that a tunnel had been constructed in 1806 under Kings Weston Road when new gardens next to the site of the hamlet were laid out. This tunnel enabled the Harfords and their employees to go to and fro without coming out into the village. In or near to the tunnel, there is said to have been an ice-house four feet thick, a not uncommon possession among wealthy families at that time.

Mr Stevens remembers that: "Mrs Harford in her wheelchair would come down to make calls on her tenants in the 'Green', as it was called then, with one of her daughters, Agnes or Charlotte. The gravel path was kept neatly trimmed to the width of her chair. They came by way of the tunnel."

The hamlet was also known as Henbury cottages. Very picturesque in the style of the Harford's dairy, and by the same architect, they were also considered functional by the standard of their times. From *A Popular Retreat*, one learns that all the cottages "had privies, ovens and coppers for washing." From Maurice Stevens: "Although we had no piped water, and a coal range for cooking, no bathrooms, and oil lamps for our lighting, we did not think we were lacking in any necessities of life, except perhaps piped water."

There were nine cottages, ten dwellings because one was a double cottage. They varied in size and design but there were features common to all. For instance, they all had large ornamental brick chimneys, which varied in number. Some had dovecotes, some were thatched, some tiled. They had garden seats and small porches/verandahs. Maurice Stevens recalls: ". . . grouped round an oval green in the centre of which is a pump and sundial erected by J S Harford's son. Each cottage has its own garden and is situated so that each doorway is invisible to the other cottages, to ensure greater privacy."

He remembers the residents back in his early youth before and during the Great War 1914–1918: "I was born in Oak Cottage in the year 1903 and lived there for 24 years. My father, Joseph Stevens went there to live after his marriage in 1899. A letter dated September 1899 says that Mr Harford is willing to let the cottage, lately occupied by a Mr Morris to my father at a rent of £5 a year, including rates and taxes. Mr Harford undertakes the outside repairs. This was increased in 1920 to £6.10s a year. Oak Cottage was then thatched. We were the only tenants in the 'green' who were not connected with the Blaise Estate, my father Jo being the village postman. His sister was postmistress at Henbury.

"Next door, at Diamond Cottage lived a widow Mrs Davis with her three daughters. The youngest, Mrs Broad lives there still. Then Jasmine Cottage where Mr Baker lived and afterwards Mr Jones, the head woodman and Mrs Jones. At Double Cottage, Mrs Davenport and Mrs Butler lived next door to each other old retainers of the Harford family, I believe. (These two and Mrs Davis and Mr Jones, I believe lived rent-free.)

"At Rose Cottage lived Mrs Latby who had a habit of wandering off now and then. My father would dash out and bring her back when we happened to see her from our kitchen window going down the steps and out of the iron gate.

"Dial Cottage – Tom George, wage 14/- per week – the coachman. I remember seeing him sat upon his box of the carriage and pair and driving down through the village from Blaise.

"Circular Cottage, Mr Jefferies, the cowman who had, I believe two sons and two daughters. One of the sons, George died only recently. When the 'Trust' modernised his kitchen, he found he had nowhere to heat the brick which he used as a bed warmer wrapped in a blanket. A neighbour, however, managed to get him an old-fashioned stone hot water bottle.

"Sweet Briar, Mr Tiley, the under gardener (who had two sons) lived there, wage 12/-. He also for a sideline did a 'walk' for the GPO around Hallen on Sunday mornings. For this job, he received the sum of 1/-.

"Vine Cottage – Mr Barrett, head gardener; his nephew, Frank lived in the bothy in the gardens at that time.

"The total population in, say, 1910 was 27 persons. All our water was drawn from the communal pump on the 'green' which never ran dry. Sometimes it failed to work, but Mr Harvey, the plumber soon got it working again. He lifted the stone flag at the rear and descended the stone steps.

"Our water was kept in an earthenware pan in the stone scullery, a tin mug was hung nearby for drinking and filling the kettle. The pan was obtained from the man who came round from time to time shouting, 'rag and bone' or 'wana-pana'. The water from the spring was so good that visitors to the hamlet would at times ask to borrow a glass and have a drink 'of our beautiful water' from the pump. There was originally an obelisk over the spring and this was replaced by the present shaft and weathercock.

"This spring water was very hard and not much use for washing. When soap was added to it, it just curdled. Rain water was collected from the roof into large water butts. Ours had rather a brown tinge to it, as it came off the thatch roof.

"The Blaise cottages were so placed that a person at their front door could not see anyone at their door – to discourage gossiping I understood. The windows were small leaded lights, alternately diamond shaped and oblong.

Thatching at Blaise Hamlet.

A 1906 postcard of the Hamlet.

"The view from Oak Cottage – A huge Elm tree stood outside the cottage in the far corner. Between us and Mr Tiley (opposite) was a Cedar tree and a large pampas grass and between our cottage and the entrance gate was a large circular bed of pink roses.

"The people in the 'green' kept very much to themselves and rarely invaded each others' houses. George Tiley, my playmate lived opposite but I do not remember ever going into his house or he into ours. My mother would call on Mrs Barrett who did dressmaking and sometimes stay for a gossip. Neither do I remember the fathers visiting one another's gardens.

"We seldom locked our cottage door, and if we went out for a period, the key was placed under the doormat as it was too cumbersome to carry in our pockets.

"Our milk was collected every morning from the dairy in Blaise. We approached the dairy through the laundry room (now the rose garden) and through the big door and down the path skirting the lawn, past the fowls' run and up to the dairy door where Mrs Jarrett was busy scalding the Jersey milk in large open pans over boilers for butter and cream. On damp days clouds of steam were billowing from the dairy door and Mrs Jarrett on those kind of days wore her pattens.

"Our lot was one pint of raw 2d, and 3 pints of skimmed for 1d. Sometimes as a special treat ½lb of Jersey butter, stamped with the Prince of Wales' feathers.

"Milk was free to anyone in the village who couldn't afford to pay for it.

"Every Christmas Eve all those belonging to the Harford clan, i.e. the tenants of the Harfords and the employees, were invited to tea in the Servants' Hall at the mansion. Carols were afterwards sung around the Christmas tree in the conservatory or in a room in the house and small presents were handed out by the Miss Harfords."

By 1943, the Harford family no longer owned the hamlet. Mr Govier who lived at Oak Cottage, explained that in about 1942/43, when the Harford grandson decided to sell the cottages, he offered the residents a chance to purchase their own homes. There seems to have been uncertainty about the upkeep of the 'green' and other communal areas. So the hamlet was offered at auction and bought as a whole for £2930 by Mr Don Hughes. Mr Hughes, an artist, had the year previously painted it. The following year after the purchase, he approached the National Trust who eventually bought it off him for the same price.

Farmer Ray remembers some of the residents in far-off days, including the Stevens family, Mrs Dance and her next door neighbour, Mr Early who was a water diviner.

The Dance Family

In about 1934 Mr Percy Thomas Dance, an engineer, and his wife went to live in Jasmine Cottage. Edith Beatrice Grace was a Hallen girl so, on marriage, she did not move far from her girlhood home. They had four sons Gordon, Donald, Royston and Alan.

Their house had two bedrooms. Some time after Alan was born, Gordon or Royston would sometimes stay with their grandmother in Hallen to make room for the rest of the family. This seems to have been a fairly common arrangement when families outgrew the accommodation available.

Before the National Trust modernised the cottages, Jasmine Cottage had one living room containing a coal-fired range. There was a very small scullery behind the living room. Behind this again was a small lean-to containing a boiler for heating water for laundry, and bathing in a tin bath. There was a lavatory adjoining the house with outside access only. Up a winding stair were the bedrooms, quite small, just about able to accommodate a double bed each, one had a fireplace. The garden, in common with the other cottages was large at the rear and sides of the house. Families were able to grow substantial crops of vegetables and fruit, and some like the Dance family also kept chickens.

In about 1970, an extension was built on to the back of the house to provide a large kitchen and a bathroom. Access to the lavatory was then made inside. Cess pit drainage gave way later to mains sewerage.

Another old resident of the hamlet, Mrs Broad of Diamond Cottage talked to Ray Govier about a few of her memories:

"My mother lived in Blaise Castle woods years ago and she went to Dorset to live and she lost her husband there and came back to Southmead to live. And going through the woods to meet one of the old neighbours, she met Mrs Harford and Mrs Harford asked her what she was doing and she told her that she was a widow living at Southmead and Mrs Harford said there was a cottage in the Hamlet and I've been there ever since.

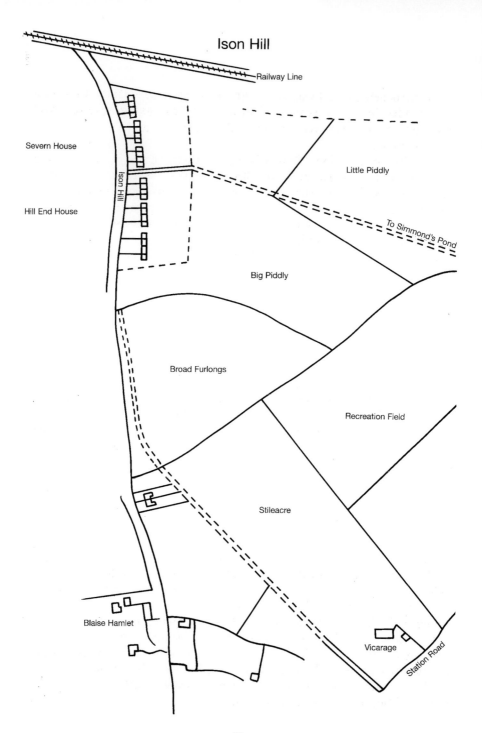

Ison Hill

Railway Line

Severn House

Hill End House

Ison Hill

Little Piddly

To Simmond's Pond

Big Piddly

Broad Furlongs

Recreation Field

Stileacre

Blaise Hamlet

Vicarage

Station Road

"I was nearly three, I was born 1906, so that would be 1909. I had two sisters. The eldest was six years older than me. The eldest was nine. And the next one, was two years younger than her, yes, and there were four years between us."

To a further question, "Now when your mother came in here, did she have any work to do at all?" Mrs Broad replied, "Not for a while, now and then Mrs Harford asked her if she would like to do the laundry work for the big house which she did. Yes, she was there for many years . . . The back of the conservatory was the laundry and she worked there for many years until the family more or less broke up."

Mr Alan Dance remembers that Mr Tom Broad was a gardener at Blaise Castle, and also looked after the putting green.

Ison Hill

Before 1920, there were no houses between Blaise Hamlet and Ison Hill. At the top of Ison Hill, the road crossed over the railway bridge and led down to Hallen. In about 1920, Gloucester County Council built a row of cottages on the Henbury side of the hill. As these were then furnished with 'mod. cons', some residents of Botany Bay moved over there.

On the other side of the Hallen Road, set well back in their grounds were two large houses, Severn House and HillEnd which enjoyed magnificent views.

In WI *A Guide to Henbury*, Severn House is described as "eighteenth century", rather similar to Blaise Mansion but smaller. In one room is a remarkable bronze fire-back. "The Estate is said to be connected with the Percival family. Spence Perceval's grandfather, first Earl of Egmont (1683–1748) was a ward of Sir Robert Southwell of Kingsweston." (There is a Southwell memorial in Henbury Parish Church.) In 1930, Captain G L Stratton M.C. was living there.

Before the Second World War HillEnd was owned by Captain Gilbert Sidney James who kept hunters and stabling in his fields.

From the time of the Second World War, these two houses underwent a series of changes. These are best described by Mr Arthur Hawkins, resident in Henbury for many years, who was very much involved in the history of Severn House and HillEnd.

Severn House and HillEnd

Arthur Hawkins was born in Brislington Village (The Rock) on 10th January 1906. His father was at that time a scaffolder in the days when scaffolds were made by fastening together fir poles with wires. Later Arthur's father went to work for the village blacksmith, and when the smith left Brislington, he became the Brislington blacksmith.

The Hawkins family were members of their Parish church. Arthur attended St. Luke's Sunday School and later, the Bible Class. His father rang bells, his mother was a member of the Mother's Union.

Arthur went to St. Luke's Village School until he was fourteen. In holidays, he went to his uncle and aunt's farm at Long Sutton, helping with all the work and learning by watching. Sometimes they would milk the cows out on the moors. He would attend competitions – ploughing, hedging – and he also joined in Young Farmers' gatherings.

In his village of Brislington was a Roman Catholic Convent. The Convent owned Wellinghouse Farm in Hallen.

Arthur's first job was working in the private garden of the owner of a market garden of 25 acres. Eventually he was in charge of the garden. This private garden had huge glasshouses for vines and roses. After eight years here, the foreman in charge of the market garden gave him a month's notice, which Arthur ignored. The owner, Mrs Marriot came out eventually and said that she could no longer afford him. He left in 1928 with good references.

He then joined Singer Sewing Machines and had to call on schools and other institutions. He sold and collected machines for repair. Minor repairs he could attend to on the spot. He also joined the Fire Service, remaining an auxiliary fireman for eight and a half years.

In 1936 Arthur married. In 1940, his parents were killed by enemy action. He and his wife went to live in Hallen. At that time he became attached to the Avonmouth Fire Service at Hemphill House North shed at the Docks. In 1940, he was taken on as a roundsman by R S Biggs of The Elms Dairy Farm. At about that time, the Convent at his home village of Brislington caught fire. In 1946, he was taken on as Bristol Fire Brigade's oldest fireman – at the age of forty! Eventually he became deaf and could no longer man the phones in the Watchroom.

In 1949/50 the Convent bought Severn House and HillEnd where they established a commercial laundry, a mother and baby hostel (at

Severn House) and a home for girls in need of moral care (at HillEnd). In 1951/52 Captain James's stables were demolished and a church was built on the site, using marble from Italy. By this time, Arthur was out of the Fire Service. The Convent laundry deliveries driver who then lived at the Lodge of HillEnd asked him, on behalf of the convent, if he could plough a field for them.

When he had done this, he was asked to plough another – and yet more. Then he was asked to sow corn for them and sowed three fields of wheat, oats and barley. He held the seed box and scattered the seed 'like playing a violin'. He was then asked to work full-time. In 1953/54 he was asked to take over the Convent's Wellinghouse Farm in Hallen – 120 acres plus 40 acres more of rented land, to rear pedigree Guernseys. The herd raised 22 milking cattle and 12 followers. He was very occupied with the Hallen herd, but he also used the Henbury land. Here, he raised cattle and sows. A lad kept an eye on these. The sows were for market. Arthur also bought cows and dealt with auctioneers.

In about 1976/77, the Convent left Henbury. The church bell went to Corsham Convent. The land was sold for house-building. HillEnd was demolished. Severn House eventually became apartments after fire nearly destroyed it.

Arthur moved from Wellinghouse Farm to the Lodge (HillEnd) where he continued to live, courtesy of the Convent who left it to him for life, in lieu of a pension.

There are reminders of the past among the new estates of attractive private houses Convent Close, Hill End Drive, Windmill Lane (old pictures show a windmill at the highest point). From there, up high, there are spectacular panoramic views.

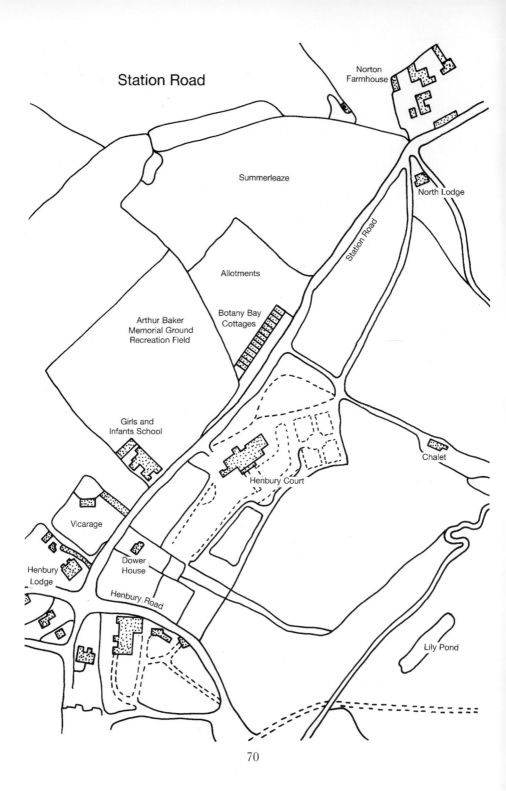

Station Road

Norton Farmhouse

North Lodge

Summerleaze

Station Road

Allotments

Botany Bay Cottages

Arthur Baker Memorial Ground Recreation Field

Girls and Infants School

Chalet

Henbury Court

Vicarage

Dower House

Henbury Lodge

Henbury Road

Lily Pond

7 – Station Road

With the coming of the railway station to Henbury, the old pack-horse lane to Gloucester, a mere grassy track, became Station Road. The heaviest traffic then was coal carts pulled by drays supplying households and businesses with essential fuel from the Coal Merchants in Station Yard.

Henbury Lodge

Today the oldest house in Station Road, Henbury Lodge stands at the corner with Henbury Road. According to the Henbury Conservation leaflet, Henbury Lodge is a large and finely proportioned eighteenth-century house. Until its recent conversion to a hotel, it still retained, almost unchanged, its original stabling and harness room. An article in the *Western Daily Press* (23.8.1986) states, "Henbury Lodge, a listed building dates back to early 1700s when it was three cottages, which were subsequently converted into one house." See also the engraving by Kip 1712.

The (New) Vicarage

Built in about 1930, this house superseded the early eighteenth century vicarage near the church and overlooking the 'dell'. Handsome and compact, it is also more functional for modern needs.

The Girls and Infants School

In the angle now made by Avonmouth Way joining Station Road, and near to the new vicarage, stood the Henbury Girls and Infants School. This nineteenth century church school was demolished in the 1950s

Henbury Lodge, now a hotel.

New vicarage, built in 1930.

because numbers were declining due to children on the ever-growing estates being sent to the new Henbury Court Schools and Blaise Primary School.

It was constructed of stone under a steep-pitched roof, and was contained within stone boundary walls with a gate opening onto Station Road. Mrs Muschamp writes: "It was a lovely old building with a wrought-iron spiral staircase. There was a tiny garden at the front containing three victoria plum trees which cropped vigorously – and did we get tired of plums!"

There was a cottage (originally the headmistress's house) near to the school entrance where villagers remember that the District Nurse lived with her sister and their white dog.

Sonia (Evans) Baynton recalls that, in the late forties, Miss Moseley was headteacher (with Mr Harris in overall charge of Boys' and Girls' schools). Miss Doreen Weekes taught the older girls and Miss K M Houlden was reception teacher. Hallen children started school at Hallen Infants and at seven went on to the Henbury schools. A number of 'Old Girls' have paid tribute to their happy school days including Betty (Woodsford) Talbot and Beryl (Love) Hill.

The following letter from Miss W Watts of Brislington throws some interesting light on the old school during the Second World War.

"I am a Home Economics teacher. I taught for one day a week (Mondays) for about three years at the Henbury School, Station Road during the war years 1939–45 in a very primitive kitchen. The old lady caretaker (the husband of her daughter was a gardener at the Somerville Gunns on the hill, I used to buy flowers from the garden) came along with her sticks and coal and lit the fire under the old copper boiler so that we had hot water.

"Upstairs (an iron staircase) was so primitive, an old iron bed and one picture on the wall was used for 'Housewifery' – cleaning the home. The dinner children had their meal at the tables in the room, and I had to talk and give my afternoon lesson against the clatter of washing up (dinner dishes) in my *only* sink. We survived and produced some good cooking from the old black Maine iron stove. The cupboards grew mushrooms as they were damp. How different from life today!

"The headmistress, Miss Williams who was not in good health did not live in the headmistress's house but in Henleaze.

"The only bus was to Westbury village so I walked from there to Station Road in the morning and back at night."

Botany Bay Cottages

Further along the road from the school, roughly where the shops were built later, stood a row of houses known as Botany Bay Cottages. No one seems to know the origin of the name though one suggestion is that having been built in the early 1800s, the name celebrates the founding of the convict settlement in Botany Bay in 1788.

Their utilities and facilities appeared to have remained unchanged for a century and a half. Harold Godfrey declares that they were condemned as unfit for habitation many years before they were demolished in 1952.

There were fourteen cottages arranged in a terrace, some single, some double-fronted. The double-fronted were numbers 3, 4, 6, 11, 12. The first eight had been built at a different time from the last six, having a different appearance. But all had long front gardens and tiny yards at the back. There was a water pump in the street outside number 6 and an emergency pump in the garden of number 6.

Mr Godfrey describes his parents' house, number 4, where he grew up, and, to which later, he brought his young bride:

"A gate led up a long front garden path to the door between two strips of garden. There were windows, two up and two down either side of the door. Inside there was a front parlour with a fireplace on one side and another front room also with a fireplace on the other side of the door. There was a kitchen at the back with a large coal-fired range.

"At the back of the house, there was a space 10 ft. deep to the high boundary wall. In this space there was, to the right, a wash-house, and to the left, a toilet, and, connected to the kitchen, a coal-house. The yard was paved with large, 2ft. square flagstones. Behind the boundary wall was some rough land and some allotments. This wall and land belonged to the Sampson-Way family.

"At Christmas, the puddings were cooked in the wash-house boiler. All the year round the weekly bath was taken in the zinc bath by the boiler that was used for the weekly wash.

"Inside the house, from the front door, a winding staircase led to the upper floor. There were two bedrooms at the front each with a fireplace, and a long, low bedroom at the back. No bathroom or lavatory! No mains water meant every drop of water had to be carried from the pump. No gas or electricity meant oil-lamps – large ones in the living rooms and small

74

Girls and Infants C of E School, Station Road, demolished in the 1950s.

Henbury Court Dower House.

4 Botany Bay from the allotments.

Godfrey family in front of the house, 1921.

ones to carry up to the bedrooms. All heating and cooking was coal-fired so coal was an important commodity."

Harold Godfrey describes how the coal was brought into the house and stored: "As there was no access in the high boundary wall at the back, coal had to be carried by the coalman through the front door, through the front room, through the kitchen where the door led left to part coalhouse and workbench (it could have been made into a small room)."

The high stone boundary wall, owned by Sampson-Ways would crack with the frost or anything else (old-age) and/or with encouragement by householders. Various gaps appeared over time, until many had access to the rough ground and allotments the other side. One enterprising family kept hens on the rough ground, while another fastened steps both sides of their wall!

They knew their neighbours well and all the children played together. But grown-ups, however friendly, never used Christian names – always Mr, Mrs or Miss! A long-standing neighbour at number 3 was Mrs Woodsford. Her son, W Woodsford lived with his family at number 13. Mr 'Wally' Woodsford was chauffeur to the Gunns of Henbury House and later chief mechanic to the Biggs of The Elms Dairy Farm. Mr Woodsford and Mrs Gunn interested themselves in and helped the Henbury Robins boys' football team of which Harold Godfrey was a young player.

Harold says he remembers the neighbours from early days, starting at number 1, the householders were William Charles Joyner, John Baker, Mrs Woodsford, Mr Frederic Godfrey, Mr Millard, Mr Harry Barnes, Mr Blackmore, Mr Price, Mrs A Hodges, Mr Rodney Talbot, Mr James Martin, Mrs G Williams, Mr W Woodsford, Mr George Goodfield. Most of these families remained at the cottages for many years. The few changes were Mr Mervyn Thomas who lived at number 2, Mr Steer at 5, Mr Bow at 7, Mr Cox at 8, Mr Sydney People at 12, Mr Charles Cullimore at 14. Later on still, Mr Sidney Tucker and Mr John Rugman took over 10 and 11.

There was at some time, an addition made to the fourteen dwellings. This is how Harold describes it: "Between number 5 and 6, there was a long shed the length of the front garden with double doors. Behind the shed joining Mrs Barnes, number 6 there was a small outhouse, I believe only one room (may have been used for stores). Mr Howell lived there, but he enlarged it, made a room at the back, and the window for this was in the boundary wall. They called this 6A when he got married."

The cottages were owned by different people and mostly rented to the householders. Harold remembers that their house, number 4 was owned by Mrs Stokes, who also owned the general stores at Hallen. Numbers 1, 2, 3 and 5 belonged to Mr Langfield, owner also of the Henbury Court Hotel.

The Godfrey family's main shopping was done in Westbury-on-Trym, walking being their mode of transport. They used Henbury village shops as much as possible because they were conveniently close by. Their lives centred round church services and church social activities. As he grew older, Harold cycled, gardened, played football, walked in the country-side, smelled the fresh country air and was happy. "Life was good!" he declared.

Hignell's Farm

Tom Hignell's parents took on the lease of Norton Farm in 1917 when the General was still alive. They were already experienced farmers from farming families. They moved to Henbury from a farm in Lawrence Weston, bringing with them their daughter, Alice Hannah and two small sons, Tom and Bob.

It was a beautiful stone farmhouse, the more recent part probably dating from the early 1800s, but Tom remembers a different section that one stepped down to and which had lower ceilings. The farmland is mentioned in early seventeenth century so the original house very probably dated from at least that time.

The farmhouse was opposite North Lodge, which was built early this century. It was demolished to build Greenlands Way and Meadowland Road.

Norton Farm covered 190 acres stretching from the farmlands of Charlton over to Piddly (Ison) Hill. About half was in the village and the rest was north of the railway line. It was a mixed economy producing both cereal crops and livestock.

After the C.P.O. (compulsory purchase order) about 1950, the farm-land south of the railway line was acquired by Bristol Council. The Hignells bought the northern section from Major Sampson-Way's Estate. They were able to continue farming for many years after that.

When their farmhouse was demolished in about 1964, the family by then consisting of Tom, his wife and their daughters, purchased and went to live at North Hill cottage, an old gamekeeper's cottage from the Sampson-Ways' time. It had been occupied by several families since its gamekeeper days.

David Hellen writes: "We lived at North Hill cottage, just behind what now is the Sun Life Sports Ground until I was about two years old (1935), when we moved to Westbury on Trym." The Hellen family had rented the cottage from the Major.

Mrs W Bryant writes: "I and my husband and eventually our two children lived at North Hill cottage from July 1948 until August 1964. In November 1947 the outlying parts of Henbury Manor Estate which lay in Gloucestershire (and so were not available for compulsory purchase acquisition by City of Bristol), were sold. We purchased North Hill cottage at that public auction."

North Lodge

High on its wall, this house bears the date 1902. It lies secluded inside a walled garden – nowadays making a startling contrast with surrounding post-war housing.

It was first occupied by Mr John Lennard, then Mr J Hunt, Beverley Marsh CH and in 1982 by Mrs Audrey Marsh.

Henbury Court

Those who remember the house, describe it as Italianate in style with formal gardens, in contrast to surrounding farmland. Within the grounds was a small chalet and at the opposite end, a stable block.

In 1827 Thomas Stock, the sugar refiner, bought The Great House at the end of Station Road. (The Great House was sometimes referred to as 'Henbury Court'. Seyer: *History of Bristol 1821* writes: "It (Great House) stood in the angle between Gloucester Lane (Station Road) and the

79

Norton Farmhouse.

Nortor Farm: the old regime.

Turnpike Road on its eastern side." Once the home of the Astry family, it had been inherited by their descendants including the Smyth family until it was sold by them in 1730, and had a period as a boarding school. Thomas Stock demolished it about 1830. In about 1807 he had built the Italianate Henbury Court in the north garden.

According to his daughter, Marianne, he lived there for 26 years and died there in 1833. The Revd. Walter Trevelyan, vicar of Henbury and a keen naturalist was his friend. Thomas was a deeply religious man and looked after ten orphans, these being nephews, nieces and grand-children. (It is a happy thought that, over 150 years later, the name of his house would be taken over by Henbury Court Junior and Infant Schools.)

In 1897 the house was owned by Admiral J H Cave, and then by Sir Thomas Lennard of the boot and shoe company who added to it a winter garden, picture gallery, music room and loggia (WI *A Guide to Henbury*). Sir Thomas is remembered as driving a coach and 'four'.

In about 1926, it became a private hotel, and then a nursery training college. During the war, when the house was being used by the Army, dances were held there which Farmer Ray remembers attending. Harold Godfrey can go back further than that. His house stood opposite Henbury Court, and he remembers watching horse-drawn carriages arriving at the hotel before the war.

Like many another Henbury house, it was demolished. This happened in the 1950s as the Council's building estate advanced along Station Road.

The Chalet

This small house, once in the grounds of Henbury Court, lay close to a right of way from Station Road, leading over a bridge and footpath to Crow Lane. It is said that Mr Arthur Thomas lived there in 1919, followed by Mr Ernest Kelly in 1935. In the 1960s Mrs Howell, District Nurse lived at The Chalet. A small community of flats for the elderly, and a warden's house have been built on the site.

Dower House

This attractively proportioned house is said to be on the site of the stable block belonging to Henbury Court. Early in the twentieth century, it was transformed into a private house.

About eleven families occupied the house between 1914 and 1976, when it was bought by Mr and Mrs Colin Bennett who still live there.

Chevening House

Another handsome house stands nearly opposite to Henbury Lodge. The earliest reference I have been able to discover is that Mrs Florence Newth lived there in 1931.

Chevening House.

8 – Henbury Hill

Chesterfield House

Some of the older villagers remember when the Aldridge family lived at Chesterfield House, in the days before the war (the family had been there since at least 1897). Miss Aldridge was Hon. Sec. to Henbury Nursing Association with Mrs Tincknell as District Nurse living nearby at Blaise Castle Lodge. After the Aldridges left Chesterfield House, a Mr Parker lived there until at least the end of the war.

Henbury Conservation leaflet describes Chesterfield House, an impressive eighteenth century house separated from the field by a ha-ha, as 'the chest of drawers' as it resembles one upside down. Its large coachhouse and stabling on the south side suffered a direct hit during the blitz. At the end of the 1960s, the empty house was badly vandalised before being restored in 1974 and a wing of flats added.

Some people recall that before restoration, it had a spell as a nightclub.

Mr and Mrs B C Hill are the present owners of the main house. Mrs Hill says she has a drawing room with a 'D' shaped end. This, she believes, was added on the advice of John Nash. The 'D' design seems to have been fashionable at the time because other nearby houses had similar additions – including Tramore, Vicarage and Vine House. Early in the nineteenth century John Nash was designing Blaise Hamlet and the Dairy for J S Harford.

The Royalls

This is now an area of parkland, part of Blaise Castle Estate. However, in the past it had been used as pastureland and, from ancient times there had been a dewpond there for watering cattle.

In the Deeds of 'Tramore', Henbury hill is referred to as, 'Royall Way'. One explanation is that from the top of the hill could be seen the 'royals' or standards of Royal Navy ships sailing up the River Severn.

Tramore

Once named 'Tramore House' and at another time 'Royall Lodge' the house goes back to the 1680s, perhaps pre-dating Henbury Awdelett. In its early life, it had several owners over time who frequently rented it out. It was not a large house but built rather for respected tradespeople and clerics.

Over the next two hundred years, it was enlarged and made elegant. The use of John Nash's window design was an indication of its standing at that time (early 1800s).

The house stands in large grounds that contain stabling, a tack room and coach-house as well as lawns and beautiful trees. A wooden covered way, the tunnel, connects the main door to a door in the boundary wall.

The Budgett family (Bristol Wholesale Grocers – H H & S Budgett) lived there for several generations before the house was purchased by the present owners, Professor and Mrs Dunn.

David believes that "the Budgetts also owned the patch of land between the Salutation and the 'Hen', where they kept hens. After the last war, when Mr Budgett returned home, he employed Mr Bray of 1 Elm Cottages to look after them. He may also have owned part of the land leading up to Chesterfield House. It is well-known that the Budgetts kept and bred Jersey cows there for export."

Mrs Betty (Woodsford) Talbot recalls that her mother Winifred started her working life in service at Budgetts. She lived in and started as an under-maid black-leading grates etc! Her wages were paid monthly and she had one day off per month. All her wages had to be given to her mother (Betty's grandmother) who was a widow, to help keep the younger children. In course of time, romance appeared in the shape of the handsome young chauffeur to the Gunns. Winifred was wooed and won!

Henbury House

A painting, oil on canvas c. 1780 in Blaise Castle House depicts Henbury House with its rounded 'wings' almost as an echo of the Castle on the hill above it. It is remembered as the home of the Somerville Gunn family who were well-known in the village as employers and philanthropists.

Chesterfield House.

Henbury House.

85

Tramore.

Vine House.

In about 1920, Mr Gunn bought The Elms pastureland from Mr Langfield. At the same time, the farmer, Stan Biggs bought the farmhouse where his family had lived since the beginning of the century. It seems to have been a happy arrangement for Mr Gunn had acquired a good investment and could look through his front windows at his lush green grass being munched by Mr Biggs' herd. At the same time, Stan Biggs was spared the outlay of money on land as well as house, and his new landlord was also a good neighbour.

One of Mr Gunn's employees was Mr W Woodsford of Botany Bay Cottages, who worked as chauffeur from the age of seventeen. Later on, Mr Woodsford also became chief mechanic to Mr Biggs when his milk delivery vans became mechanised. He was always called 'Woodsford' by the family. The Gunns were good employers, liked by their staff; they would lend the Woodsfords a car for their family holidays.

Mr and Mrs Gunn involved themselves in village affairs. Mrs Gunn was also a great supporter of the Henbury Robins football team. Mr Gunn was President of Henbury cricket club that used the Arthur Baker Memorial Ground in Station Road for their matches and practice.

During the Second World War, Mrs Gunn turned part of her house into a nursing home for the A.T.S. and one of her cottages into a 'forces' canteen. She herself helped with the nursing. Some of the villagers remember her as a very strong character. She was obviously an excellent organiser.

They lived in a beautiful large house with coach house and stables, and an orangery. A tunnel was built under the main lawn to enable gardening staff to reach the kitchen garden without being seen from the house. There may also have been, at one time, an ice house. The Gunns had a gardener called Albert Woodsford (related to Mr W Woodsford the chauffeur) and also a Mr A Williams. Another employee at one time, according to a street directory was Mr Lawrence Hawkins who was groom to H S Gunn.

David Hellen remembers going to a garden fete at Henbury House which had a fine garden with a ha-ha. His parents went to tennis parties there when they were young and single.

The building, thought to have been a kitchen joined to the house by a covered way, was during the war used as a canteen for Service personnel. It is now a private house named, 'Canteen Cottage'. However, it is thought to pre-date Henbury House. This looks like more evidence that older buildings were not always demolished but incorporated into the new as properties were 'upgraded'. It was also not uncommon to accommodate the kitchens in a separate building so that cooking smells were isolated from the house.

The gardens of the house stretched down towards 'Endcliffe'. Between the two houses was (still is) a path leading to the Tunnel Field (the tunnel under the vicarage garden). Behind the high stonewall of the Gunn's garden next to this path was their stableyard and a cottage. Many villagers remember when the Albert Woodsford family lived there.

Vine House

This was the original and present name of 'Endcliffe'. According to the Henbury Conservation leaflet: "It was built in 1725 with stone quarried from what became the cellar; later extensions were made with stone quarried near the end of the garden."

J D Pountney, founder of the Bristol pottery was born there. "At one time he owned a pottery at Westbury, called the Sugar House Pottery, where the chimney pots and ornamental bricks for Blaise Hamlet were made, as well as the moulds used by sugar-refiners." *Pountney: Old Bristol Potteries* (page 222)

Vine House has a magnificent garden falling away down to the brook. Professor and Mrs Hewer, who lived there for about 50 years until 1996, created the beautiful gardens using many rare plants from home and abroad.

David remembers when it was the house of the Stainer family. (They are thought to be related to the composer of Stainer's *Crucifixion*). The Stainers bought their groceries from Mr Hellen's shop in Westbury. Around 1940 David and his father would call at the back door of the house in the morning for the order and deliver the groceries in the afternoon. Few of the big houses had telephones then.

The Salutation Inn

Next to Vine House stood the inn. Farmer Ray remembers this inn from his early youth when he would stay with his grandfather William

Canteen Cottage.

The old Salutation Inn.

McEwen Smith at Westmoreland Farm. The building well known to them was an earlier version than the present one.

Ray's memories go back to the end of the Great War 1914–1918. His grandfather would walk with him round the ford, in those days almost constantly flooded. Horses pulling heavy loads would be watered there by their carters; ducks and swans dabbled and swam. Mothers and small children would come out on warm summer evenings to feed the birds. The fathers would walk round, like William to quench their thirst and greet their cronies at the inn.

Small Ray would be sent out to the back to sip his lemonade sitting on a bench by the warm boiler. He enjoyed these outings even though grandfather spent his time chatting with his friends. Ray felt part of the country scene, and part of this was the old Salutation, small, ancient, friendly. It was then managed by Mr Ruddock, who was a tenant publican. When the new Salutation was built in the 1930s it had a new Manager, Mr Wilfred Ironside, who remained there until after the war.

David Hellen remembers that when he was a boy, Mrs Ironside was the landlady. Brian Frost's mother would often be helping at the inn when David and his father delivered groceries there in the 1940s.

The old inn stood not far back from the ford bridge. It was a popular meeting place for farming folk and did not have the restrictions then imposed on the Porter Stores.

Henbury Hill House

Climb back up Henbury hill. There, at the top, almost opposite Chesterfield House stands Henbury Hill House. Whoever decided to build here must have been attracted by the magnificent views across Henbury to the River Severn. Said to have been built in late Georgian times, it has an interesting small tower and a curved balustrade facing the road.

The WI booklet informs one that "for many years in the last century it belonged to Arthur Baker, a corn merchant who used to ride on horseback from his house to his mills on Redcliffe Back." The Arthur Baker Memorial Ground in Station Road was given to the village in his memory by his family.

The gardens extended along the Ridgeway for twenty one acres. Beyond these grounds in gardens once belonging to Brentry House stands the gothic ruin known as the 'folly' or 'look-out' beloved of local children years ago. The WI booklet records: ". . . mock-ruin, a church window set between two rubble towers. The window was originally the west window of the Lord Mayor's Chapel in Bristol. In 1822, the Common Council took this down and put a copy in its place. The old window, a fine example of the 'late-decorated' period was given to a member of the Council, Mr J Cave, who built it into a stone screen in his garden." (Could J Cave have been an ancestor of Admiral J H Cave who, in 1897 sold Henbury Court to Sir Thomas Lennard?)

The original west window of the Lord Mayor's Chapel.

1931 *Kelly's Directory* lists Mr Percy Steadman in occupation of Henbury Hill House.

The house later became the Junior House of the Clergy Daughters School, headmistress Miss Almond.

In the war it became a Government Hostel for the A.T.S. After the war, the Methodist Church, who then owned it, used it as a temporary Theological College until the purpose-built Didsbury College was completed in the grounds.

Miss Watts remembers: "The Army were billeted in Didsbury College. I remember one morning hearing crying and sobbing. I looked up to see a young eighteen-year old soldier at an open window sobbing his heart out."

Cottages on the hill

Along Henbury hill, just inside the wall of Henbury Hill House, there used to be a cottage and coach-house round a stable-yard. After a fairly recent fire, two new houses have now been built on the site.

There is another cottage further down the hill, called 'Beech Tree Cottage'. I believe there were one or two other cottages in the vicinity before 1950.

David Hellen recalls that his friend, Brian Frost lived with his parents in part of Chesterfield House. Later, they went to live at 'Beech Tree Cottage'. This is also listed in *Kelly's Directory* for 1950. (David remembers playing in their garden.)

In the directories for 1939 and 1947, Reginald Charles Dredge is listed as living at Henbury Hill House Cottage.

Mr Harold Godfrey recalls that his brother-in-law, Mr Cecil Houldershaw lived at 'The Cottage'. The 1950 directory also lists this information.

David remembers that: "Below the cottage (Beech Tree) was a fairly large Market Garden [now Didsbury Close?]. This was run by the Jefferies family (Mr F H Jefferies). The grounds extended back a long way with a walled orchard at the rear. The house itself was set back from the road up a short drive, with more trees in the front."

Clifton Cricket Club

David says: "Just below the Market Garden was a large field, where Arnall Drive is now, and a gate led into this just adjacent to the drive. A notice on the gate said 'Clifton Cricket Club'. There was a hut of sorts at the edge of the field, and you could make out the playing square. Of course, I only knew this from 1943, and I never knew of anyone playing there."

The Elms Dairy Farm

Most people knew it as 'Biggs' Dairy'. Part of the view from Henbury Hill House included the pastureland where Channel Island cows grazed peacefully, and from where milk carts (later, vans) carried hygenically-processed milk from the dairy by way of a team of roundsmen. The Biggs family bred their own cows, made their own hay, processed their own milk and other dairy products. They finally had it all conveyed to the doorsteps of nearby villages and to the suburbs of Bristol.

The house was regarded by the family as dating from Queen Anne's reign. Other authorities say "a fine seventeenth century farmhouse with eighteenth century additions." So, like many of its neighbours, it 'grew'. Described elsewhere as a "lovely typical Cotswold farm", it faces uphill and is a pleasant sight as one walks from the top of the hill down Henbury Road.

The Biggs family took the lease of The Elms in about 1900. During their three generations, they created and maintained a herd of Guernseys on a forty acre pasture, installed a "state of the art" dairy and, at its greatest, had a team of twenty roundsmen.

Biggs' Employees

Ray remembers Richard (Buller) Croker who was a roundsman for Biggs. It has already been mentioned that Mr Woodsford became Stan Biggs's chief mechanic after his delivery carts changed to motor vans.

Another employee of very long standing was Mr Teddy Love. He was born in 1905, the eldest of four brothers and a sister (who died in infancy). They grew up at Berkeley Cottages in Charlton Lane just across Passage Road from the Crow Inn. When Ted was eleven, his father was killed in the Great War. He then took over responsibility of head of his family, and sought and obtained work at Biggs Dairy.

93

The Elms Farmhouse in 1907.

Elm Cottages and Sparside.

He was a pupil at Henbury Boys' School in the Close, and had to obtain permission from the Headmaster to arrive late in the mornings so that he could help with milking. He started as a general farm-worker haymaking, moving cattle etc.

Later on, Ted became one of Biggs' roundsmen, first driving a trap with churn and ladle. Later came milk bottles, and in about 1930, he delivered milk and dairy produce by motorised van.

When Ted married, he and his wife went to live in Hallen, Moorhouse Lane in about 1929. In about 1934, they moved to Blaise Hamlet. Their two children attended the Infants' School in Station Road. Beryl went on to the Girls' School there and left at fourteen. Denis went to the Boys' School like his father before him. Just before he reached the top class, the leaving age was raised to fifteen. Then, when Granny Love became old and ill, they moved back to Berkeley Cottages to be with her.

Ted's daughter, Beryl says that her father's life was entirely a countryman's life. Born in the cottage near Passage Road surrounded by farmland, he was brought up to be honest, upright, and hardworking. From the evidence of his behaviour after his father's death, he also exhibited a strong sense of responsibility.

Elm Bungalow

This bungalow is set back from the road behind Elm Cottages. It was built in about 1920 by Mr Somerville Gunn to house his chauffeur and family. This was after Mr Gunn had bought The Elms farmland.

A Mr Pounsberry lived there with his family at one time. According to a letter that Mr Poundsberry wrote to the *Evening Post*, his sons worked at the stables of Henbury House. These were approached through a wooden gate near the present entrance to Henbury Garden flats. There were hunters and ponies which they rode into Westbury to Jim Grigg the smith.

A villager remembers that at another time, the bungalow was occupied by a Mr Kettlety and his family. Some time after the war, it was bought by Mr Robert Biggs who greatly enlarged the accommodation, and who lived there with his wife and family.

Georgian Cottages

There is a row of terraced cottages – 1 & 2 Elm Cottages and 1 & 2 Sparside – opening on to Henbury Road opposite to the Salutation Inn. Elm Cottages are double-fronted and two-storied. Sparside Cottages are single-fronted and three-storied.

Elm Cottages have a 'communal' extension at the back, now separated. Mr Powesland thinks that it may once have been used in communal work such as laundry, weaving, sewing, mat-making. Cottage industry has traditionally supplemented agricultural wages, and women can more conveniently work at home.

For many years number 1 Elm Cottages was the home of Charles Bray, a jobbing gardener working for various people, including Mr William Budgett. David Hellen says that his granny (in the Corner House) would know when he was on his way to the village as he would always sing hymn tunes as he walked up Church Lane.

The Powesland family lived at Number 2, from 1930. Today it is still occupied by a member of that family.

In Chapters 2 and 5 it has been explained that Mr Francis Powesland was employed by Dr K Wills, along with the circumstances of the family's arrival at Elm Cottages. It is understood that Dr Wills bequeathed the house to Francis Powesland after long and loyal service. The children had moved away but after the death of Francis and his wife, the youngest son, Peter returned and bought the house from his father's estate.

At one time, the family rented a room to a Dr Hooker so that he could run a GP surgery for the village. Decades later, family members still refer to that particular room as 'the doctor's room'.

Sparside Cottages

Farmer Ray recalls the villagers who lived in these houses in the 1930s and 1940s: "Mr William Jones was at number 1 Sparside, and I believe there was a well with spring water somewhere in house or garden. Billy lived there with his wife and two daughters. He worked for William Budgett of Tramore, as cowman. Mr Budgett kept pedigree Jersey cows behind his house. This herd was inbred to keep the stock pure. He sold his calves abroad, to Africa and all over the place. I well remember his fierce bull. Even though it was kept tied up, I would keep my distance!

"Next door lived Charles Williams with his wife, son and daughter. Charles worked as carter for Dick Willis of Hallen, a farmer and hay-dealer. Dick bought and sold hay, you could say he ran a hayfarm. Charles' son Frank was known as 'Lanky' among his friends. He worked for me on my farm for a short time. Later he went to work for Teddy Knee at a farm on the Mendips. Their mother sadly died, and Charles' daughter kept house for her father and brother."

Fane Cottage

For many years before the Second World War, Fane Cottage was the home of Mrs Annie Hort, sister to William McEwen Smith who was Farmer Ray's grandfather. Mrs Hort, a farmer's widow returned with two of her children to Henbury, the village of her birth after her husband's death. Her daughters, Gladys and May became close friends of the Rowles girls and the Biggs family as well as with their McEwen Smith cousins. May married Reg Pearce a farmer from Lawrence Weston. Gladys, after her mother's death, married Cleeve the Ironmonger.

The cottage is thought to be seventeenth century and at one time a cooperage, where barrels and kegs were manufactured.

'Fane' was the family name of the Earls of Westmoreland. In 1638, the Countess bought tithes including those of Henbury. In 1639 she gave them to her son, Sir Francis Fane.

9 – Crow Lane

Westmoreland Cottage

Traditionally a farmworker's cottage tied to Westmoreland Farm, in the 1930s Westmoreland Cottage housed an employee of the Sampson-Ways. Probably originating from the seventeenth century and then quite small, in recent years it has been much extended and enlarged.

A Mrs Clifford writes about the cottage from her personal experience:

"My husband's family were living in Westmoreland Cottage when I first knew them in 1936. Their names were William and Kate Clifford. They had four children, Mervyn (my husband), Stanley, Hilda (who is living in Australia) and Ronald. William was head gardener for Major Sampson-Way and when there were weekend guests, Kate used to help in the kitchen. Just after I was married, the Cliffords moved to the bungalow near St. Mary's.

"My husband was great friends of the Rugmans who lived near Blaise, especially Charlie Rugman.

"William was one of the bell-ringers in St. Mary's, and Kate was a regular churchgoer.

"If my memory is right, I think the Porter Stores used to be a pub and my husband's father used to go there once a week generally on a Saturday evening."

Westmoreland Farm

The oldest part of the house is almost certainly sixteenth century; some ceiling beams may have come from Spanish Armada wreckage, about 1588. Over succeeding centuries, there have been additions of adjoining barns/top storeys and byres culminating in early 1800s with the addition of a substantial high-ceilinged wing at right-angles to the earlier part.

The limestone, partly honey-coloured bakery/dairy building behind the house probably dates from the seventeenth century. The majestic

Old Westmoreland Farmhouse.

Westmoreland stables and barn.

99

Westmoreland Cottage.

The old Crow Inn in 1950s before being demolished for major roadworks.

barn and stable block faced with dressed grey stone has been described by one architect as 'in the Palladian style.'

Henbury tithings were purchased in the 1630s by the Countess of Westmoreland, so it is reasonable to suppose that they were collected in this barn and possibly from an earlier period. It is also possible that the old farmhouse itself started life as a thatched 'one up/one down' to house a 'keeper of the tithe'. (When restoring the house, the present owners found large traces of thatch in the roof space.)

The farm was on land granted to the Sadleir family, later passing to the Astrys, then Smyths and their descendants until at least the end of the eighteenth century. The Tithing map indicates that by 1830/40 the Sampson/Sampson-Ways certainly owned the land and tithes.

To explain the above two paragraphs: "After the seizure of church lands by the Crown in the 1540s, the tithes often became separated from land ownership. So that the Countess of Westmoreland owned tithes but never owned the land here."

Since the mid-nineteenth century, the McEwen/McEwen Smith family became tenants of Westmoreland Farm and remained so until the compulsory purchase order in 1950. Robert McEwen, born about 1820 was the first of their family to farm here. He was succeeded by his son William who married a Miss Smith from the Midlands. They then changed their name to McEwen Smith. William inherited a thriving farm, and seems to have enjoyed a good standard of living, employing two domestic staff as well as the usual farmworkers, carters, cowmen, labourers. When Ray was a boy, just after the Great War, the house was already provided with electricity and mains water. William's income enabled him to bring up four daughters and a son in relative comfort.

At the time of William's death his only son already had his own farm and it was decided that his grandson, Ray should take on the tenancy. Ray was seventeen years old, and the story of how he fared is an important part of *Lost Farms of Henbury*. In the 1990s, Farmer McEwen Smith and his wife still live in the farmhouse.

Their land stretched from the Ridgeway alongside The Elms pasture over to Passage Road, to the Station and along the brook back to the ford – 148 acres in all. They reared cattle, sheep, pigs, fowls, cereal crops and hay. The family had always kept ducks and swans on the brook and on the ford, it was a pretty sight, a noted beauty spot. The McEwen Smiths' land spread both sides of Crow Lane, along which were hedges and ditches to prevent animals from straying. Every few years, hedging had to be carried out (to keep the hedge under control) and the ditches had to be cleared frequently.

Before 1950 Crow Lane was a muddy cart-track giving access to the farmfields, and enabling friends to visit between Henbury and the hamlet of Brentry. Brentry children also took this route to school.

Lily Pond

Just behind where the modern swimming bath stands, there used to be a lily pond, created and stocked with lilies and fish by the landowners, the Sampson-Way family.

It seems to have frozen over quite often in the winter months, and everyone appeared to enjoy the fun, young and old, the 'gentry', their employees, their tenants, shopkeepers, tradespeople, professional people. The Sampson-Ways themselves would drive across the fields with a carriageful of guests for the skating.

In summer, the swans would sometimes get onto the lily pond. Mushrooms grew round it in abundance; early morning mushroom gatherers could be seen in Lily Pond field. The cows grazed peacefully round the pond. It was a typical rural idyllic sight!

On such occasions of enjoyment, the classes of society seemed unimportant.

The Crow Inn

Crow Lane also gave access to the Crow Inn. Quoting from the WI *Guide to Henbury*, ". . . possibly a late sixteenth century inn . . . It may have been a coaching inn for passengers from Wales, as it stood near the important main road which led from Bristol to Chester. The South Wales cattle drovers, using the old grassy tracks from Aust, must have drunk their ale there." Describing this ancient and interesting building, the article continues, "Its two gables, stone-mullioned windows, thick stone walls and heavy beams suggest the word 'old' as part of its name but strictly speaking it should still remain The Crow Inn as it certainly was in 1750".

The WI article describes the broken clay pipes dug up in the inn garden as a reminder of the time when "a new pipe was provided free for every customer and thrown away after use". "There was also a hitching post on the outside wall. The old brewhouse with its tall copper used to stand in an outhouse near the stables".

An article in the *Bristol Evening Post* dated April 15th 1959 includes a picture of this old inn. The article reports that it was known to locals as, 'The old Pecker' and Mr H G Hignell says that his grandfather held the licence in the 1870s.

In 1892, the inn was said to have been closed down after pressure from some influential Brentry citizens. It was thereafter a private cottage until reopened by the brewers Watney Combe Reid and Co. in June 1955.

Late in 1959, the old inn was demolished for road-widening and the Brentry traffic roundabout. It was then replaced by another inn that is known as 'The Old Crow'. A picture taken just before the demolition shows the ancient and the modern inns side by side.

In *Lost Farms of Henbury* a mistake was made in describing the householders between 1892 and 1955 as 'landlords'; for this, I offer deep apologies. I understand that Mr Jennison carried out a great restoration job on the cottage.

10 – Passage Road and Wyck Beck Road

Before Westbury started an extensive building and road-widening programme in the 1930s, Passage Road was very much a country road leading to the 'Passages'. The houses along it were few and scattered, some of them quite ancient. One of these, on the Henbury side of the road was George Hignell's cottage and shop. There were also a few farmworkers' cottages and, across the road was Brentry Lodge, home of Mr Charles Farr. High on the hill above Brentry Lane stood classically-inspired Brentry House, one-time home of Mr J Cave. For many years this century, the house has been used as a hospital.

With the widening of the road, more houses appeared. Along the edge of Henbury, from Ridgeway to Railway there were now about thirty two houses, including a post office. Over the road north of Brentry Lodge were fifteen new houses.

About the same time, Wyck Beck Road was created in the grounds of Wyck Beck House. A 1940 Directory lists eight houses as follows: 'Brent Beck' occupied by A S G Grey; 'Tylsdale' by Thomas Till; 'Leigh Delamere' by George E Pearce, 'Flitching' by William Oates; 'Arden' by George Hamilton; 'Cradley' by Morris Coates; 'Wayside' by Bertram Jutsum; 'The Cabin' by Sidney Cottrell.

In nearby Brentry Lane there were a few old cottages, a handful of houses in Knole Lane and several farms in Brentry. Brentry people walked or rode over to Henbury for many purposes – to the shops, church, schools, – to see friends.

Sonia Baynton who, as a child, lived in Brentry Lane remembers this part of Henbury/Brentry. Her grandfather was Mr George Pearce of Leigh Delamere whose house backed onto Wyck Beck House garden.

She recalls that the Misses Dunford ran the Brentry post office and sold sweets (still rationed in the late forties). Mr B Jutsum is remembered as having a smallholding in Charlton Lane. A family remembered in Passage Road was Jackie Lane's family. Jackie married Ken Lane, landlord of the 'King William' in Hallen. Her grandparents, Harold and Edie Makey lived at Wyck Beck House and were friends of the Jennisons of the 'Old Crow'. The Rugmans lived in a cottage opposite the end of Dragonswell Road. Tom Rugman was a farmworker on Westmoreland Farm.

11 – Passage of Time

The Great War

Some villagers can just remember the Great War 1914–1918. Henbury families who were bereaved then included the Love family whose beloved father was killed. Harold Biggs was badly wounded, and lost a leg. Shells caused death and destruction, and trench fever also claimed many lives. but apart from the shelling of a few coastal towns, civilians did not come under fire in that war.

The war years gradually receded from people's memories and soon the twenties arrived. Women's skirts shortened, so did their hair. This accompanied an enormous change in attitudes about women. Many had worked in weapons factories, earning better money than domestic service could provide. Women were being educated, they were having smaller families. With enfranchisement, they were beginning to voice their own opinions on matters usually thought to be the preserve of men.

But in rural villages like Henbury, there was little change of life-style and only a small amount of mechanisation until the late 1930s. In Henbury, the country bus became a bit more frequent and there were a few motor cars. The village remained a close-knit community. The Second World War radically altered this state of affairs.

Second World War

In the Second World War, there was great injury to civilians as well as to service people. Hardly a hamlet escaped, and many towns, cities and industries were badly damaged.

Because of an ever-present fear of invasion from the air, each area of the country had a 'Home Guard' Unit on alert around the clock. Industrialised areas were major targets of enemy bombing but, partly due to defence measures e.g. camouflage and blackout, bombs were mis-directed and fire bombs were dropped to help enemy pilots to get their bearings. Nowhere was entirely safe.

In rural areas such as Henbury near vulnerable industries and factories, searchlight batteries and anti-aircraft guns were installed. Civilian defence involved air raid shelters, gas masks, blackout, removal of road signs and a system of Air Raid Wardens. Church bells were silenced, to be rung only in the event of enemy invasion. To carry out these measures able-bodied people were recruited for Home Guard, Air Raid Warden, firefighting services and installation of shelters. Farmers were under government contract to produce greater and greater amounts of food. Exactly what they grew was decided by the Ministry of Food.

Numerous units of service personnel came into the village to man the searchlights and guns. Young Henbury men and women were called up to the Armed Services. Some of the school children were evacuated to safer places away from the Bristol area.

A few villagers have provided their own experiences of Henbury at war. Tom Hignell and Ken Lane joined the Home Guard together. In the early days, their duty area was Spaniorum Hill. They had between them one pitchfork and one shot-gun (but no ammunition!). Ken remembers that later on Tom would come down from his home at Norton Farm by bike. They would then walk to the hut at the end of Bank Road, and along the Severn (guarding the tunnel approach), mainly from Bank Road, between Severn Beach and Pilning and over to New Passage. The rifle range at New Passage was used for their practice and they did eventually have rifles and ammunition for their duty.

Once, early in the war, they were on duty at Hallen crossroads in the pitch-dark blackout when they saw a brightly lit bicycle speeding towards them. They called out, "Keep that light down, there's a war on!" A very angry voice shouted back, "Mind your own business. How dare you young newcomers to my village tell me what to do!" As he sped past, the young men realised that this was Farmer Wallace, Head Air Raid Warden of Henbury and Hallen!

Peter remembers that Major Sampson-Way organised the Henbury Air Raid Wardens. Ray was one of his group. They patrolled various parts of the village, Ray covered the centre. Their job was to check the blackout, coordinate any rescues and keep their headquarters informed.

Farmer Ray remembers devastation of his stock and buildings from fire and other bombs, and the night Mrs Biggs's hen-house caught fire. With many others he witnessed the catastrophic bombing of Filton. They also watched the terrible strafing of Bristol City and Avonmouth Docks.

Air Raid shelters were issued to families who had at least one child under the age of fourteen. These Anderson shelters were half-buried in the garden and, packed around with sand bags, they tended to become water-logged. The Powesland family were rescued from their water-logged shelter by the major. Peter, in common with some of the other children was evacuated for a short time, but didn't much enjoy the experience. It was a difficult task for organisers to match families to children under all the strange and frightening circumstances. There were also public air raid shelters, one on Canford Park, another in the Harford's tunnel.

Several villagers remember tank traps, intended to impede enemy movement in the event of invasion. These 'traps' took the form of a series of rectangular little manholes, each with a metal cover about 2 inches by 9 inches, about 2 feet apart and in two or three rows. In use, the lids would be removed and iron girders dropped into the sockets, thus creating a barrier of iron posts. There was a set of them at the major's back door (between Henbury Lodge and the Salutation), and a set at the top of Hallen Road as you turn into Kings Weston Road.

There were also 'bird tables', a gas-warning device; a post about 4 feet high with a flat wooden top painted lime-green. The presence of gas would change the colour.

Villagers recall early in the war when the hill between the railway line and Berwick wood was being dug out for installation of the petrol tanks; and many recollect the searchlight on the Arthur Baker memorial Ground in Station Road and the anti-aircraft gun on the Showground behind the ford.

There were A.T.S. in Henbury Hill House, and a convalescent home at Henbury House, where Princess Royal paid them a visit. The American Army was at one time billeted in Kings Weston Park in Nissen huts among the trees, and probably also in the House itself. One villager relates how they used to tip their rubbish in the overgrown woodland between Lawrence Weston Road and Greenhill Lane. "I recall walking there one evening on a family outing . . . and being astounded at the food, and especially crates of rotten oranges that had been disposed of."

As war dragged on, the village filled with newcomers, mostly service people. There were dances at Henbury Court Hotel; the Carlton cinema flourished in Westbury. Popular radio shows increased. The old 'wireless' cheered everyone with ITMA, Monday Night at Eight, Variety Bandbox and Children's Hour. The bus service improved, running now from Westbury to Henbury, Hallen and Brentry.

The farmers working harder than ever, lost their farmworkers to the 'call-up'. In their place, landgirls were employed. Tractors largely took over from horses. Engine power had taken over on the streets also. The war hastened this transition so that post-war, the remaining horses were mainly dray horses pulling heavy load such as beer barrels and coal.

As war proceeded, news filtered through to some of the families – dreaded news of the death of a loved one. This was a grievous time. Henbury's fatal service casualties included Percy Newman, Dick Clifford and Wally Rudge.

12 – After War – The Homecoming

After the Great War, council house building programmes had throughout the country provided houses and flats for rent suitable for returning servicemen and their families. In general they were well-built of good quality materials. Ison Hill cottages date from about that period.

After the Second World War, housing had radically decreased due to extensive bomb-damage and a war-time moratorium on house-building. Thousands of young people of marriageable age were being demobilised from the armed services. Authorities urgently cast round for suitable areas for housing. Some bomb-damage sites were used but many were in inner cities where the bombed houses had been small and inadequate, hence the appearance of high rise blocks where many could be accommodated on a small area. Much more was needed, so new greenfield sites were purchased and where necessary, they were compulsorily purchased.

In Henbury, the coincidence of this urgent need with the death of the largest private landowner has been described in some detail in *Lost Farms of Henbury*. From about 1950 onwards rural Henbury gradually gave way to suburban Henbury.

As this war ended, David Hellen was twelve years old. He writes: "Some of us remember that Mrs Gunn of Henbury House had 'Welcome Home' banners attached to the railings of her house. Many other people put up these notices on the front of their houses. Sometimes it was 'Welcome Home Frank' (or whoever).

"Then there was the 'Henbury Welcome Home Fund'. Mr Charles Hellen (my father) was Treasurer. It was set up in October 1944 to create a fund to distribute to returning servicemen. Chairman was the Rev. J C Lloyd, Hon. Sec. was Mr W J Ubank and it was registered under the War Charities Act. Eleven collectors were appointed and by January 1946, £674 was collected. The 248 who qualified in Henbury Parish received £2 and 10 shillings each.

"The Newmans of Raglan Villa had a room at the side of their house (at one time Charles Newman's office). This was used for small gatherings, and I went there for the V.E. Day party that was organised for the village children . . . we had to take our own cutlery, with identifying wool tied on the handles. We were given a commemorative mug, a plain white mug onto which had been hand-painted in red and blue (red, white and blue), a large 'V' and . . . – (morse code) – and the first time it was washed, all the paint came off!"

An American Soldier

After the war, one American soldier returned home with his Unit very reluctantly, for he had fallen in love with the Henbury countryside and with a local young lady! He returned, married his sweetheart and they settled in the area. He still loved to walk, and he became very knowledgeable about this part of Bristol. He and his wife reared their family, eventually becoming grandparents. His widow, Mrs Patricia Edmead has lent some of her husband's pictures for this book.

New and Old Henbury

For nearly fifty years, new Henbury has settled down. The first young families have grown up and grown older. Second, third and even fourth generations have been born. To children in Henbury nowadays, Henbury is an old suburb, and they probably cannot imagine it any other way.

Henbury children know Blaise parkland and woods. They play on the grassy banks of the brook. Some hedges and ditches remain from the farmland. Quaint old buildings contrast with modern housing. Old Henbury is hidden within new Henbury but everywhere clues to old Henbury can be found. Perhaps this book will help younger people to discover it and older people to recall their own memories of it.

RESOURCES AND ACKNOWLEDGEMENTS

The author wishes to acknowledge with thanks the help derived from the following:

Contributors to the book (from their memories)

Mrs S Baynton (née Evans)
Mrs W Bryant
Mrs A Claxton
Mrs Clifford
Mrs G Dance and her family
Mrs E Day
Mrs J Dunn
Mrs P Edmead
Mr H Godfrey
Mr R Govier
Mr A Hawkins
Mr D Hellen
Mrs B Hill (née Love)
Mr D Hough
Mr T Hignell

Mrs P Jacob
Mr K Lane
Mr D Love
Mr R McEwen Smith
Mrs P Mitchell (née Newman)
Mrs H Muschamp
Mr R Pearce
Mr P Powesland
Mrs B Rideout
Mrs J Steele
Mrs P Stevenson
Mr F Talbot
Mrs T Talbot (née Woodsford)
Miss Watts
Mr M Stevens (through Ray Govier's transcript)

Books

Eveleigh D *A Popular Retreat* (City of Bristol Museum and Art Gallery, Kingsmead Press, 1987)
Layzell D *Invitation to Henbury* (Redcliffe Press Ltd, Bristol 1984)
Nicolson A *Life in the Tudor Age* (Readers Digest Ass Ltd, 1995)
Oxford History of England various books Clarendon Press
Rudder S *A New History of Gloucestershire* (first published 1779)
Wilkins H J *Ecclesiastical History of Westbury on Trym* (J Arrowsmith Bristol & London, 1909)
Hallen & Henbury W.I. *A Guide to Henbury* (F Bailey & Son Ltd Dursley, 1970)
St. Mary's Church Leaflet *A Brief History*

Photographs have been kindly lent by many contributors mentioned above. City of Bristol Museums and Art Gallery have lent photographs from their collection. Two photographs are from the collection of 'Bygone Bristol'. Mr & Mrs R Hood kindly sent the pictures of 'The Window'. It stands in their garden.

Maps	Bristol Records Office
Ordnance Survey Diocesan maps	Henbury Rates Books, maps & other documents

Thanks also to: Blaise Castle House Museum for permission to copy and use Mr Govier's transcripts of Mr M Stevens' memoirs; Bristol Central Library for photocopying and unfailingly courteous assistance; Henbury Library for continuing friendship and support; Mrs Jean Tonkin and Mrs Beryl Shaw for help and encouragement.